Grand Illusions *

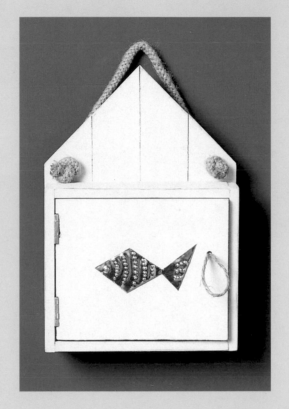

Grand Illusions*

Paint Effects and Instant Decoration for Furniture, Fabric, Walls and Floors

Nick Ronald and David Roberts

Photographs by David Downie

T

Trafalgar Square Publishing

For Caroline

First published in the United States of America in 1997 by
Trafalgar Square Publishing,
North Pomfret, Vermont 05053

Printed and bound in Italy by New Interlitho Italia S.p.a., Milan

ISBN 1-57076-071-3

Library of Congress Catalog Card Number: 96-60772

This book was conceived and designed by
WORDS & PICTURES
31 Napoleon Road, St Margarets, Twickenham TW1 3EW

Editorial Direction Joanna Copestick
Art Direction and Design Meryl Lloyd
Design Assistant and Typesetter Ian Muggeridge
Photography David Downie
Photographic Assistant Miranda Daymond
Photographic Styling Meryl Lloyd, Nick Ronald

PAINT NOTES
Please note that the paint names quoted throughout the book relate to
Grand Illusions' own range of new generation water-based paints. They are
available by mail order. See page 130 for addresses
of Grand Illusions and other stockists of water-based paints.

Contents

Foreword

When we first started our company we wanted to project our own personal image, one which was true to ourselves rather than one which had an overly commercial edge. To this day we still buy from the heart. Call it an instinct if you like. Accessories for the home should embrace good design, integrity and style without being elitist. By following our instincts we have, over the years, developed a certain inimitable style and reputation by offering products which we believe in.

In this book we offer our ideas on home decoration. People often try too hard to accommodate what fashion dictates, mixing and matching ready-made coordinates which can rapidly usurp creativity. In truth, we should allow our creativity to flow. Apart from a few basic ground rules, there is no real recipe for combining the elements that will make your home. As long as you are sincere, you are more likely to realize your vision.

The same ethos applies to our decorating techniques. Although not necessarily a definitive collection, we believe that they meet the criteria described above and are pared down to the best essentials. A veritable cornucopia of ideas working harmoniously with one another. We hope that you use this book as your primer and let your imagination do the rest, because, as Einstein said: 'Imagination is more important than knowledge'.

Simply Grand

Oh Happy Day! Just what you needed, yet another book on paint effects. Well, just for the record, we are always being asked to recommend a good book on this subject. While there have undoubtedly been some inspirational ideas within the covers of many a decorating book, few contain everything we wanted to know, and many were either too long-winded or too specific and technical. How many times have you skipped the first few chapters of a book, having only bought it for the projects at the back?

With this in mind, our book is designed to be entirely practical, short on superfluous technicalities, but fabulous to look at. It also aims to encompass the decorating preoccupations of the nineties, where time and resources are precious commodities. We have created projects which are at once colorful to look at, quick and easy to make and, where possible, made from non-toxic, recyclable materials.

Besides, we like to think that we have something original to say. We've certainly created some new techniques and brought several traditional ideas right up to date. Most importantly, we've taken note of what our customers have been asking us for.

Some books will tell you that color should be used with caution. Some books will tell you to stick to tradition and paint a small, dark room with light bright colors rather than work with what you've got, with gusto. *This* book allows you to follow your heart and confirms that color is an uplifting experience in all its forms. And yes, white is a color too by the way. It's a scary thought that as recently as two generations ago, access to color was extremely limited. Nowadays, thanks to huge technical advances in print and paper production, we're almost blinded by color and the choice can be intimidating and at times, overwhelming.

Even quite recently, if a paint company launched a "traditional" paint range, it invariably offered a collection of beige and other muted tones. While boasting historical accuracy, these insipid palettes were not exactly inspiring. Thankfully, as the world shrinks with the advent of cheaper international travel and multimedia technology, we can *all* travel from the comfort of our armchair and discover that "traditional" now encompasses the vibrant colors of South America, the sherbet hues of the Caribbean and the hot, spicy tones of India and Mexico.

And paint has moved on too. We've taken the marvel of latex one step further. Nowadays, one can of the new generation of water-based paints will work in a myriad of ways. Diluted, it can be used as a woodstain or colorwash for a wall. Or you can use it straight from the pot to form a flat, matte covering. Burnished with steel wool, the paint will produce a resilient shine, while sanding it back will reveal a variety of tones within each color, thus creating an illusion of age. These paints offer all this *and* are ecologically sound and odorless. Our projects are a testimony to their versatility.

During the next 144 pages we also touch on two other key areas of interior decoration: texture and individuality. We show how to paint fabrics and floorcloths, create instant mosaics and apply 3-D relief to walls using nothing more than paper and card. Never lose sight of the fact that you are decorating for you, your family and friends. In this world of mass-produced ephemera, cherished memories of a transformed junk-shop find make a room unique. Wit, in the form of something unexpected, has a welcoming effect and great charm. After all, remember, your home is one of the few places where you can do exactly as you wish.

Our influences are sometimes obvious and sometimes merely a nugget of information, visual or otherwise, gleaned from a picture, a place or a person. From Matisse to Madras, our sources are wide and varied. The Mediterranean is a rich font of ideas, but so too is the simple country look from around the globe – an eclectic mix if ever there was one. Inspiration is all around us in the form of color, pattern, shape and mood; in magazines, books and films.

If we were forced to use just one word to describe the contents of this book, 'simple' certainly sums up the majority of the decorative techniques we have created. We believe that all our projects have visual integrity, yet they have all been made using the most basic of everyday materials, from string to grout, paper to paint. Above all, despite the simple techniques, every project is believably professional; in other words, the ultimate Grand Illusion.

Where possible we have stuck to basic equipment when devising our projects. Many of the materials and tools you will require should already be in your tool box. This is a guide to the more specialized items you may need, most of which are available from craft shops, artists' suppliers or your local home center.

Safety Note

When cutting wood or sharp material such as tin, do take extra care. Use protective gloves and anchor your work in a workbench or secure it to your worksurface with a clamp or wooden battens before commencing work.

Paintbrushes

Our projects call for a variety of brushes, many of which you will probably already possess.

Artists' brushes
Small brushes useful for areas of fine work. They are available in large, medium and fine sizes. We tend to use large and medium versions.

Stencil brush
A soft, hairy brush which is ideal for transferring details onto walls and objects.

Stippling brush
A stubby stencil brush used to stamp on detailed decoration.

Household paintbrush
Used for painting walls and wood. Available in a large range of sizes. Always soak brushes in warm water to clean them.

Wallpaper paste brush
We tend to use these thick, bristly brushes for some of our wall-painting projects. They are easy to use and help create an irregular finish.

Paints and Varnishes

Our own Grand Illusions new generation of specialist water-based paint provides a matte finish for wood and walls. It produces a more attractive finish than conventional latex, which is also water-based. However, the vinyl in regular paint forms a skin when dry and therefore does not sand back well. One gallon of Grand Illusions' paint will cover approximately 14 square yards.

Our paint can be watered down in various ratios of paint to water to form a colorwash applied over a base coat of pale, solid color. It adheres brilliantly to wood and can also be used on walls, as long as it is protected with a coat of water-based lacquer or varnish to seal in the color. For examples of color combinations, see Color Palettes on page 131.

Acrylic gesso
Gesso is a white primer which hardens as it dries, strengthening the object to which it is applied. After using gesso, soak your paintbrushes in warm water immediately for ten minutes or so, then wash them in soapy water and dry thoroughly.

Acrylic raw umber
An artists' paint, raw umber comes in a tube and can be diluted to form a "dirty wash", for ageing objects.

Gilding paste
Also known as gilding cream, this "instant gilt" comes in a tube or a glass jar. Used sparingly and applied with a finger or a soft cloth it provides a touch of gold to several of our papier mâché projects.

Craquelure varnish
A water-based varnish system which cracks as it dries on a painted surface to create a broken patina.

Water-based floor varnish
A strong, durable varnish which will protect and toughen painted floors, whether wood or concrete.

Satin-finish water-based varnish
A final coat of satin finish water-based varnish will protect and enhance wooden surfaces as well as walls. It dries to a satin sheen finish and makes the surface wipeable.

Shellac
A natural varnish and sealant which dries to a very durable sheen on wooden surfaces.

Wood

Softwood
All our projects call for planed or sawn pine which is readily available in home centers. Where pre-cut sizes do not suit your requirements, larger stores should cut wood to any size for you. Most pine stocked by large stores is now obtained from sustainable sources, although some of our projects could be tackled with old wood you may have lying about in your garden shed. Old floorboards and shabby pieces of junk furniture are ideal for recycling into decorative pieces for the home.

Doweling
Wooden doweling is available in varying lengths and diameters.

Wooden skewers
Small wooden sticks which we have used to make masts for our Ocean Liner and as makeshift needles for threading string through lampshades and fabric.

Papier Mâché Materials

Posterboard
A stiff, white card available in large sheets from artists' suppliers. It is stronger than cardboard and is eminently suitable for our 3-D papier mâché projects.

Electrical cording
Cheap and widely available from hardware stores and ironmongers, electrical cording comes in a variety of widths. Strip the inner wires from the cord with a scalpel before using it to form rims or edges on objects.

Modeling material
At last, a mass-produced alternative to the conventional paper pulp which is laborious and time-consuming to make. Modeling material comes in cheese-like slabs, is inexpensive and has a dough-like consistency. We used it to form decorative motifs for our Pulp Sculpture Plaque and feet for our Papier Mâché Bowl.

Glues

Latex-based white household glue
A white glue, also known as rubber solution, which is strong enough to stick paper, card and light fabric. Most importantly, it contains latex (rubber) which is a vital ingredient for our distressing techniques on terracotta and wood.

White household glue
A light household glue used to stick paper and fabric. When diluted 1:1 with water it acts as a sealant.

Epoxy-resin glue
A very strong glue suitable for sticking tin and metal. Always wear protective gloves when applying epoxy resin. We used it for our punched tin projects.

Repositionable spray adhesive
A strong glue for paper and card which comes in an aerosol spray. Use it in well-ventilated areas.

Tin plate
Also known as galvanized steel sheeting, this is available from specialist suppliers.

Tools

Miter saw
Although it sounds a little technical, a miter saw is an inexpensive piece of equipment which will open up huge possibilities when it comes to cutting wood. It is basically a clamp-cum-saw which allows you to cut wood at any angle. We used it to create our own picture frames.

Electric jigsaw
Useful for cutting wood into thick shapes, a jigsaw should ideally be used with a workbench.

Awl
A small "dibber" which makes holes in wood prior to nailing or screwing.

Center punch
Another useful little object which is the mainstay of our punched tin projects. Center punches come in different sizes. When gently hammered against tin, they will create a small indentation.

Wire cutters
Or "indoor secateurs" which will cut tin plate.

Basic Paint Techniques

Here are the basic paint techniques which we use singly or in combination for many of the projects in the book. We have applied them to several picture frames so you can see what the end results look like. These techniques are perfect for virtually any color combination and any piece of wood, from picture frames to chairs, tables to wardrobes. The use of new generation water-based paints creates a rich texture and many different tones within the flat color once it is sanded, giving the impression of many more layers of paint. Please note that these techniques do not work with regular latex paint, as it contains a plastic skin which will not sand back in a satisfactory manner.

Two-color Ageing Method One

This is the paint technique in which you see elements of the base coat showing through the top color to suggest wear and tear and an aged appearance. It is shown here with water-based Jaipur Pink paint over a base of Caribbean Blue.

Method

Here is a brief summary of the method used to create this effect. For a more detailed description, see the projects listed right. If using new wood, stain it first. For wood which is already painted, sand it to create a key. Apply two coats of your base color, allowing each to dry thoroughly. Once dry, paint on one or two coats of your top color and allow to dry. Next, sand back the surface to reveal haphazard elements of the base color. Concentrate your sanding on edges, feet and knobs and areas where wear and tear are likely to occur. Ideally, finish off with a coat of wax for a really professional look. Or seal the surface with shellac, water-based lacquer or satin varnish.

We used the technique for: Two-color Aged Chair (page 26), Striped Frame with String Trim (page 42), Peg Rail (page 22), Ocean Liner (page 52)

Two-color Ageing Method Two

A similar technique to Two-color Ageing Method One, this gives a more mottled look, less subtle than Method One. It is shown here in water-based Caribbean Green paint over Cornflower Blue. This effect is suitable for virtually any color combination on any piece of wood. As before, steel-wool, when applied to the whole painted area, will bring out many different tones within the flat color.

Method

Follow the same preparation as for Two-color Ageing Method One then apply two coats of your base color, allowing each one to dry thoroughly. Where you wish to see elements of the base color exposed, use a candle to rub haphazard candlewax over those patches. Paint on one coat of your top color and allow to dry. Use grade one steel wool to rub the top-coat and reveal areas of base color where the wax has been applied. Finish off with a coat of furniture wax, or seal with shellac, water-based lacquer or satin varnish.

We used the technique for: Painted Urns (page 34), Picture Frames (page 42)

One-color Ageing and Distressing

Basically the same principle as Two-color Ageing, but where only one color is required and a varying degree of base wood needs to be shown. It is seen here applied with water-based Cornflower Blue paint. This technique works well on both large and small pieces of furniture and even on terracotta pots and urns. It gives the impression of a credible battering. Always apply glue haphazardly to ensure good results.

Method

Stain new wood before you use it, or work on old boards. Apply haphazard patches of latex-based household glue where you want the wood to show through – normally edges, feet etc. Allow to dry thoroughly. Paint on one or two coats of your chosen color, allowing each one to dry thoroughly. Next, sand the wood back to reveal the patches of glue and then pull it off by hand. Continue to sand until the required amount of wood is showing. Finish off with a coat of wax or seal with shellac, water-based lacquer or satin varnish.

We used the technique for: Picture Frames (page 42), Pot Board Table (page 28), Aged Mirror (page 32), Painted Urns (page 34)

Basic Paint Techniques

Raising the Grain

This is a wonderful way to transform brand new pine into a tactile piece with a distinctive grain and pattern. While fairly dramatic as a technique, raising the grain produces deep grooves on what was previously very flat and ordinary wood. If liming is not to your liking, then this technique also beautifully enhances one- and two-color ageing. To raise the grain use a blow-torch to gently char the surface of the wood on all edges which will be visible. (Below left). Using a wire brush, move up and down the grain to brush out all the black dust. (Below right). Clean the surface with a damp cloth. The wood is now ready for painting or staining.

Raising the Grain and Painting

The technique is shown here two-color aged in Apple Green and Yellow paint. It is suitable for either new or waxed softwood (pine). Wood that has been treated with heavy duty lacquer and varnish must be stripped first. Make sure that your wood is solid pine and not pine particles, which is often used for economy shelving sold in home centers. Raising the grain and painting is wonderful for mirrors, picture frames, shelves, table tops or for any pine piece that needs a texture. It's even suitable for pieces which are waxed, as the technique removes the wax at the same time.

Method

Raise the grain as described above. If after cleaning with a soft cloth, a lot of dark patches remain, tone these in with a coat of water-based woodstain and allow to dry. Next, one- or two-color age in the normal manner.

We used the technique for: Bathroom Cabinet (page 50), Ocean Liner (page 52)

Raising the Grain and Liming

Liming is not normally associated with pine, as the grain is not pronounced as it is in oak or other hardwoods. However, like raising the grain, liming can transform softwood, producing a finish similar to that of driftwood. You can also achieve the same result using liming paste, a tricky chalky paint which, when dry, is rubbed with steel wool. This requires sealing with satin varnish. Instead, try white paint wiped on with one cloth and wiped off immediately with another one. This technique is perfect for small pieces like shelves, mirrors, picture frames and small cupboards. Take care on larger pieces in case the end result looks patchy.

Method

Follow the instructions for Raising the Grain and Painting. Next, apply liming paste with a cloth or brush, working a small area at a time, and rubbing the wax into all the grain. Leave for 2-3 minutes and wipe off with a clean cloth. Buff up to a sheen. Repeat as necessary to increase the limed effect.

We used the technique for: Bathroom Cabinet (page 50), Picture Frame (page 44)

Raising the Grain and Colored Liming

This is virtually the same effect as limed pine except that a colored tint used as a base provides a pale coloring for the piece. We've shown it here with a blue wash under the lime. The other two methods for liming mentioned above are fine for this effect as well. Liming can only be applied after a coat of shellac or satin varnish has sealed in the color.

Method

Follow the instructions for Raising the Grain and Painting, although staining is highly recommended too. Mix your chosen paint color in a ratio of 1:1 to water to create a wash and apply this to the wood. When dry, seal this in with a coat of shellac or satin varnish. Apply liming paste with a cloth or a brush. Concentrate on a small area at a time, working the wax into all of the grain. Leave for 2-3 minutes, wipe off with a clean cloth and buff to a sheen. As before, repeat as necessary until the desired amount of white paste remains embedded in the grain.

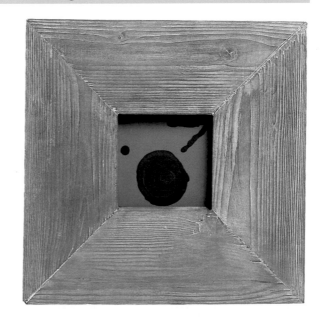

We used the technique for: Picture Frames (page 44)

Basic Paint Techniques

Craquelure

Craquelure, (not to be confused with crackleglaze or peeling paint medium) is where the varnish or lacquer cracks over a painted surface, rather than the paint itself cracking. Until recently, craquelure was a tricky substance to use and the results were variable.

Method

The following is based on a two-part water-based craquelure which is available from any good artists' supplies shop or specialist paint stores and home centers. Paint the chosen piece as you wish and allow to dry thoroughly. Apply the craquelure base coat with a soft brush. It will be milky in appearance, so smooth out any obvious brushmarks. When the base coat becomes clear, it is ready to receive the top coat – it will still be slightly tacky. Brush on the top-coat, smoothing out any distinct brushmarks. As the top-coat dries, fine cracks will appear. When completely dry, "dirty up" the cracks by applying undiluted raw umber, wiping off any excess immediately with another damp cloth. Seal with satin varnish or lacquer.

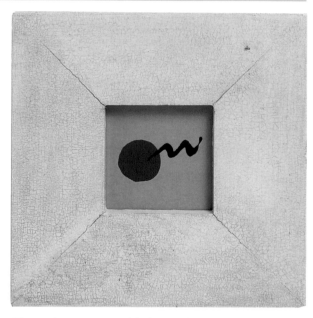

This technique is suitable for small painted objects such as candlesticks or terracotta pots.

Milky Sheen

We always commence our paint courses with a technique we call milky sheen. In some ways, the word "technique" is too strong a description for what is basically a demonstration of how our specialist paint performs differently from regular latex. It gives a pale milky hue and a satin-like sheen.

This finish can mark with frequent handling, so is most suitable for picture frames and small objects which are designed to look good rather than be put to practical use. You can maintain the softer color by applying water-based satin varnish, although some of the satin-like sheen will disappear.

Method

Paint your chosen piece in a minimum of two coats of one color and allow to dry thoroughly. Take a plastic scourer (industrial grade is best) and gently rub up and down in the direction of the grain. The paint will immediately take on a white hue. Buff up to a sheen with a soft cloth.

We used the technique for: Picture Frames (page 45)

The Effect of Waxes

Undoubtedly, the most professional finish for any painted piece is a coating of furniture wax. It gives a rich, deep shine and is highly durable. Although waxes come in many varieties and brands, essentially they fall into two types – petroleum-based and non-petroleum based (water-based) – the latter being more eco-friendly and, as a consequence, harder to find. They tend to come in four main shades:

Clear – contains no pigment so will just intensify the color of the wood rather than change it.

Honey pine – has the slightest of brown tints which just seems to make the final result brighter and crisper than the clear version on most colors.

Antique pine – has a distinctive brown pigment in it that is released in a haphazard manner to give an impression of "antique" pine. It will "dirty-up" most paint colors and has an excellent effect on natural wood.

Black wax – The darkest of them all, and it is very dark! It will make natural wood turn a very dark shade of brown and when used with color, will intensify it to its darkest shade – for example, it will turn navy blue into a really deep midnight blue.

Waxes provide a hard, durable shine and will also clean and remove an element of paint when used in the two-color ageing process. While waxes would be our preferred choice of finish, they do not work well in a wet environment such as a kitchen or a bathroom. In these cases you should use water-based satin varnish, lacquer or shellac.

Wax intensifies paint colors. Therefore, you should always test on a sample board first. It is not so noticeable on white or darker colors, but certainly affects the paler ones dramatically. It works particularly well on old wood.

Method

Apply a coat of wax sparingly with a soft cloth such as muslin, working on a small area at a time. Allow to dry for 5-10 minutes and then buff with another soft, clean cloth. For large areas consider buying a waxing brush attachment for use with an electric drill.

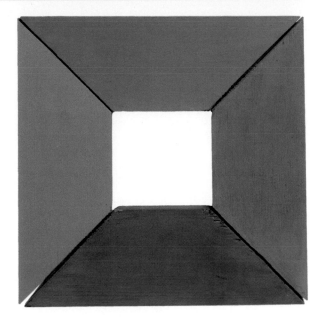

The four main shades of wax: Clear (left), Honey pine (top), Antique pine (right), Black wax (bottom), over Provence Blue paint

Water colors

It would be impossible to write this first chapter, or indeed the book, without commenting that the discovery of our own specialist water-based paint has transformed our lives, not just commercially, but spiritually too.

A combination of natural and earth pigments in the paint provides a magical quality, colors work in harmony with one another and the result is a mellow effect which can be sanded back easily to create a faded look.

Color is undoubtedly the key – the *joie de vivre* of the piece. Never be confined by tradition – color is as personal a statement as you can get. Nowadays it's not just flat color either. It's two-color combinations, where an element of the base color shines through. It's liming, it's waxing, it's broken color, it's cracked surfaces ... it's glorious.

Paint Matters

In the 18th and 19th centuries, journeymen decorators had to make their paint from whatever raw materials they could find – dairy products and skimmed milk were often the medium; brick dust, yellow clay, vegetables and berries were the likely pigments.

Milk, while being a most effective paint medium, is not a commercial proposition these days, as its shelf life is too short; in modern times it has been replaced by an acrylic medium. However, the glorious qualities of milk paints remain in the new generation of specialist water-based paints; they offer a rich chalky texture without producing the vinyl skin of regular latex. Their other outstanding quality is an ability to adhere to bare wood without the need to prime it first, so that the character of the wood is preserved. No wonder then that these new paints based on old recipes are ideal for restoration and rejuvenation alike.

Paint has got to be one of the most underestimated decorating materials for walls, floors and furniture, yet it is probably the easiest to use. There is no quicker, more economical or versatile way of putting your signature on your surroundings. But we're not talking walls of flat color using latex paint here. We're talking about washes of color that offer transparency and depth, or patterns and tones that can recreate the texture of uneven stone. Major transformations can be achieved with little effort and skill.

As paints go, the new generation of specialist water-based examples are front runners. You can dilute them to make a woodstain or use them as a base for colored liming. You will see how easy and effective this paint is for one- and two-color ageing. The subtle tones that are released when wood is sanded back create the perfect illusion of age. You will also see how a humble kitchen scouring pad can produce a milky sheen. In a similar manner, when the paint is burnished with steel wool it produces a fine polished sheen which is both attractive and durable.

Another decorating "miracle" is raw umber, which is an artists' water-based acrylic paint or "instant ageing in a tube" as we call it. This mud-colored paint, when diluted with water, dries in a suitably haphazard manner which is perfect for "dirtying up" or giving an aged patina to painted surfaces.

Similar effects can be achieved with other artists' paints such as Burnt Umber, Raw Sienna and Burnt Sienna.

Most importantly though, the beauty of these paints is that they minimize preparation and drying times. Wood requires no priming if painted with this type of water-based paint and floors just need to be sound and dry before you start your decorating work.

Our colorful journey begins with a project which is a gently aged, two-color Shaker peg-rail and leads on to a series of chairs treated in the same way. The photograph of this project on pages 24-25 shows more than sixteen colors working together, in combinations so rich that the chairs nearly march right off the page!

We then look at "distressing" – the term often used to describe the paint-ageing process. To our minds though, this term is more appropriate for treatments in which you want elements of the bare wood to be exposed. We include small-scale objects such as a mirror made from old floorboards (page 32) and also show the same technique applied to a large piece of furniture, our heavy pot board table (page 28).

Finally, to show you just how versatile this sort of work is, we apply the same principles to ageing and distressing terracotta, to produce a result reminiscent of faded French olive jars (page 34). So, say goodbye to Magnolia Land and a big hello to the Paint Zone.

Two-color Ageing

We hesitated about using the word "ageing" for our two-color ageing process, but decided in the end that the final result does look like most people's idea of an aged paint finish. In reality it is a paint technique which allows elements of the bare wood and base-coat to show through the top coat. The surface is then sealed with wax or shellac to give a truly satisfying and professional finish. It certainly gives an aged appearance, but its virtue is the combination of two disparate colors, which can look utterly traditional or crisply modern.

Painted Peg Rail

All the participants in our regular paint courses take home with them a peg rail treated with their chosen paint technique. Shaker-like in appearance, it is a useful yet attractive object that really benefits from two-color ageing. Here we chose a top coat of Antique White over a Terracotta base — perfect for a kitchen or a bathroom. If you want the peg rail to hang in wet environments remember to seal the surface with either a water-based satin varnish or lacquer rather than furniture wax.

Materials and Tools

Water-based wood stain, medium or dark
Water-based paint, Terracotta and Antique White
Clear furniture wax
Medium-grade sandpaper
Two soft cloths
1 in paintbrush

1 Staining and Painting the Wood
Stain your wood with a water-based medium or dark wood stain. Allow to dry then paint on two coats of the base color (Terracotta) and allow to dry. Apply one or two coats of top color (Antique White).

2 Sanding and Waxing
Sand back slowly and gently along the grain to reveal the base coat underneath. Apply clear wax sparingly with a soft cloth. Wait for 5 minutes then polish the surface with another cloth.

Two-color Aged Chairs

Here we've used our two-color ageing technique on a rush-seated ladderback chair using two distinctly contemporary colors – a Provence Blue base coat with a bright Jade on top (see page 132 for color palettes). The result is a very attractive piece indeed, which would be equally at home in a Caribbean kitchen or an English conservatory.

Materials and Tools

Water-based paint, Provence Blue and Jade
Water-based woodstain, medium tone
Clear furniture wax
2in paintbrush
Medium-grade sandpaper or steel wool
Soft cloth

Previous page A collection of rush-seated ladderback chairs and a smaller wooden chair demonstrate the vibrant color combinations achievable with our water-based paints.

1 Wood Staining

Stain your wood to prevent any traces of new wood shining through when you sand back later. Water-based stains are easy to use, odor-free and eco-friendly. Allow to dry thoroughly before painting.

4 Sanding Back

Start sanding in the direction of the grain to reveal the base coat. You will notice different tones appear within the top color, providing a pleasant grained effect and allowing the luminous blue to shine through.

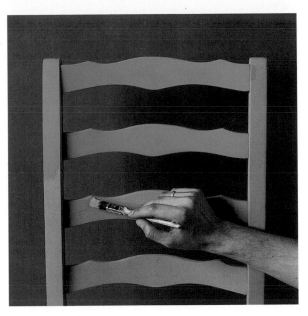

2 Applying the Base Coat
Next, apply one or two coats of your base color. We have used a Provence Blue here. Apply the color evenly all over the chair using a 2in paintbrush. Darker colors need two coats for good coverage.

3 Applying the Top Coat
When the first color is completely dry, apply one or two coats of your chosen top color. We have used a single coat of bright Jade here to provide a rich and colorful Mediterranean feel.

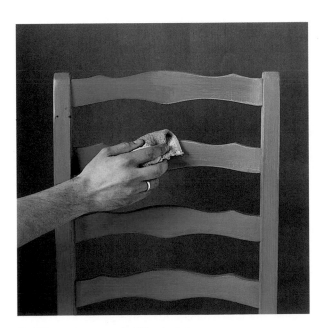

5 Waxing and Finishing
Wipe the chair to remove any dust left from the sanding process. Take a small amount of wax and spread it on evenly. Leave for two minutes, then polish it up to a nice shine using a soft, clean cloth.

6 The Finished Effect
This kind of two-color ageing can be made to look as traditional or as modern as you like. It's all down to your choice of color combinations. See pages 132-137 for a collection of color palettes.

Pot Board Table

Here is our heavy pot board table in all its glory, looking distinctly baronial with its two-color ageing and heavy distressing.

This piece of furniture, rich in color and texture, looks like it has seen life, yet is wonderfully contemporary too, providing a strong focal point in any room.

If the colors are too bright for you, try a subdued top coat of Antique White applied over a Buttermilk base. The richness of the natural pine tabletop against the neutral colors would make the table fit perfectly into any naturally-oriented scheme.

The crackleglaze we used here is available commercially and is applied between the two colors – it is a little tricky to use, as only one brushstroke is permitted when applying it. Crackleglaze medium is very sensitive to temperature and air pressure, so it can be temperamental. If you have not used crackleglaze before, always experiment first on a scrap piece of wood.

Materials and Tools

Latex-based household glue
Water-based paint, Cornflower Blue and
  Caribbean Blue
Crackleglaze medium
Two soft cloths
Antique pine furniture wax
Medium-grade sandpaper
Two paintbrushes, one 1½in and one 1in

Previous page A pot board table, heavily aged and distressed, provides baronial elegance and a chance to display precious objects.

1 Applying the Glue

Apply haphazard patches of glue to all areas where you want wood to show through. Concentrate on the edges, sides, knobs and feet of the furniture. Allow to dry for at least 2-3 hours.

4 Applying the Top Coat

Now paint one coat of Caribbean Blue all over the base coat. Take care as you apply paint over the crackleglaze medium, as you can only use one brushstroke to apply the paint.

2 Applying the Base Coat
When the glue is dry, apply the Cornflower Blue base color over the same area. Leave the top of the table clear for waxing later.

3 Optional Crackleglaze
For areas where you want a peeled paint effect, apply a generous coat of crackleglaze medium with a 1 in brush. Leave to cure for a minimum of four hours.

5 Sanding Back
When the paint is completely dry, sand back as desired. The glue will appear as transparent patches and these should be peeled off by hand. Smooth-in the peeling paint with a light sanding.

6 Waxing and Polishing
Working on a small area at a time, apply the wax to the top of the table using a soft cloth. Wait for a few minutes, then buff to a shine with a new cloth. Wax the rest of the table in the same way.

One-color Ageing

One-color ageing and heavy distressing works extremely well on picture frames (see page 40), furniture (opposite) and mirrors. Here we've taken a mirror whose frame is made from old floorboards and painted it in Antique White, heavily distressed it and finished it off with a coat of wax.

The secret is to apply haphazard patches of latex-based household glue, just like we did for the Pot Board Table on page 28. When the glue is completely dry, apply two coats of paint, having carefully masked off the glass mirror first.

Old floorboards also make wonderful pieces of furniture such as small cupboards or shelves. Their authentic recycled appearance means that they are perfect for painting too. See page 13 for more information on one-color ageing and distressing.

Materials and Tools

Water-based paint, Antique White
Latex-based household glue
Clear furniture wax
Medium-grade sandpaper
Two soft cloths

Opposite A French *meuble à farine* one-color aged in Antique White provides light relief in an all-white interior.

1 Removing the Glue
When all the paint is dry, gently sand it back with medium-grade sandpaper – this will reveal the dried glue which should be peeled off by hand as shown.

2 Finishing Off
Wipe the frame with a damp cloth to remove any loose paint and then apply the clear furniture wax with a soft cloth. Leave to dry for a few minutes and buff to a shine with a new cloth.

Painted Urns

These decorative urns take their inspiration from the faded olive storage jars that grace many a French antique shop, from Marseilles to Monaco. We decided to apply our distressed, two-color ageing paint technique, most often used on wood, to terracotta urns and pots – and were thrilled with the results.

To create a waxed paint surface which is a passable alternative to conventional ceramic glaze, we coated a terracotta urn with a haphazard layer of latex-based household glue. It perfectly resembles a faded or chipped glaze.

For these urns we always apply a base coat of Antique White, water-based paint. It seems appropriate but is by no means an essential element.

Materials and Tools

Medium-grade sandpaper
Clear furniture wax
Latex-based household glue
Water-based paint, Antique White and
  Cornflower Blue
2in paintbrush
Household candle
Steel wool
Two soft cloths

1 Distressing the Surface
Apply the glue haphazardly to create an irregular pattern below the rim, above the base and around the middle of the urn. Add similar patches to the two handles. Allow to dry for 2-3 hours.

4 Sanding Back
Gently sand the surface with medium-grade sandpaper to reveal the glue. Peel it off by hand. Use steel wool to burnish the top coat and remove the candle wax, revealing the base below.

2 Applying the Base Coat

Apply Antique White paint starting at the pot rim and working over the patches of glue. Do not paint the area in between. Rub a candle haphazardly all over the base coat to act as a resist.

3 Applying the Main Color

Once the candle wax has been applied and the base coat is completely dry, after about one hour, paint the same area with a coat of Cornflower Blue. Allow to dry thoroughly.

5 Wax Finish

When you are happy with the amount of sanding and burnishing you have done, apply clear furniture wax with a soft cloth and leave for a few minutes. Then buff up to a shine with a different, clean cloth.

6 Faded Grandeur

A combination of two paint colors, a coat of latex-based household glue and a covering of candle wax are all that are needed to create a gloriously colorful aged finish.

Woodworks

Given that buying and rejuvenating junk-shop oddities is rapidly turning into a blood sport — you, versus the wily antique dealer — we thought that there was a call for ideas on how to create your own decorative naïve pieces. Objects that have all the charm of days gone by and, just like their predecessors, are made with the simplest of tools and a mere lick of paint.

The appeal of such handmade accessories relies more on your interpretation than any technical skills, more on your sense of fun and enjoyment of color, than any fine art degree or woodwork experience.

We'll show you how flat, new pine becomes mellow driftwood, rope and tin become decorative accessories and a kitchen scouring pad is used to create a milky sheen on wood. So, relax and enjoy, you'll discover how wood works.

If you like Scandinavian painted furniture or the clapboard charm of New England buildings, then you'll enjoy the next few pages. Don't be put off by the title of this chapter. You don't need to be a carpenter or possess a degree in engineering to accomplish these projects. Thankfully most home decorating stores will now cut wood to size for you. Most of the projects call for pre-packed planed or sawn softwood, such as pine. Even if you cannot find the exact sizes, you should be able to produce the same effect with a little bit of measurement-tweaking.

Softwood is available everywhere now and most home centers buy their wood only from sustainable sources. Home centers are usually more expensive than lumber yards, and in our experience, quite often lack the sophisticated cutting equipment which we rely on.

We mostly use planed boards which have a smooth finish. Sawn boards are rougher and softer. In their natural state they will not accept paint as easily as planed boards, due to their rough edges and flaky surface. You can also use old, bought or found pieces of wood for these projects. Packing cases, orange crates, tea chests or junk-shop furniture are all great sources of interesting wood, depending on the project. Old floorboards are wonderful for making clapboard-type furniture, as is new tongue-and-groove panelling, tacked onto a simple frame.

All the projects are small-scale, so there's no call for a well-equipped workshop before embarking on any of them. Just use a sturdy table or kitchen unit. Cover it with a dust cloth and a large piece of MDF (medium-density fiberboard) to form a makeshift workbench.

The only substantial (although not expensive) tools you will need are a miter saw for the Ocean Liner and an electric jigsaw. They are both easy to use but care should be taken with the jigsaw, as with any electrical device. A free-standing workbench may be useful (and safer) when you are working with an electric jigsaw.

So, if you like the style of the Shakers – uncomplicated, simple and clean, then you should appreciate the naïve pieces we've prepared for you. We'll show you a whole range of picture frames (pages 40-45), putting into practice the techniques described in Chapter One. One-color ageing and distressing, two-color ageing with some embellishing, plus two new ones – craquelure and milky sheen – all applied to picture frames which are made with the wonderful miter saw.

We'll introduce you to a small handy key cupboard (page 48), which should be the starting block for all manner of similar pieces. Pride of place in this chapter though is the exciting Raising the Grain technique used on the Bathroom Cabinet (page 50) – see page 14 for further details of this method. This incredibly straightforward procedure will lend grain and texture to any flat piece of pine – instant ageing courtesy of a blow torch, if you like – but perfect for painting or liming too, as you see fit.

And lastly, the same technique is used to make a glorious Ocean Liner (page 52), normally made from weatherbeaten driftwood but we show how to transform bright new pine into faded, aged grandeur. More than ever, this chapter is designed to inspire you to greater things. Make pieces that appeal to you, be it colorful whim or faded treasure. This is your chance to exercise your creative muscle.

Overleaf A collection of simple wooden frames treated with several of our paint techniques demonstrate a glorious array of styles.

Our striped blue picture frame takes the two-color aged theme one step further with embellishments of string and cockleshells. Follow these simple rules and you cannot go wrong:

✻ To avoid recesses, always build the inside of your frame to a size which is just a little smaller than an existing clip-frame size. That way, the backing and glass of the pre-cut clip frame will fit neatly behind your frame and can be secured in place with a simple picture fixing or even strong tape.

✻ To keep the frame square when gluing, use a specially designed picture framing clamp or fix two wooden battens to your worksurface – nail them to one another at 90-degree angles.

✻ Smaller-diameter moldings or wood are more likely to cut accurately than larger ones. However, any irregularities can easily be fixed with filler.

Materials and Tools

Planed pine pre-cut as follows:
2 x: *11 x 2¾ x ½ in
2 x: *9 x 2¾ x ½ in
*cut to a 45-degree angle

Wood glue — Satin varnish or wax
Wood filler — (optional)
Water-based paint, — Miter saw
  Antique White — Electric drill
  and Provence Blue — ¼ in and ³⁄₁₆ in
Jute string —   drill bits
2 cockleshells — Pencil
Medium-grade — ½ in paintbrush
  sandpaper

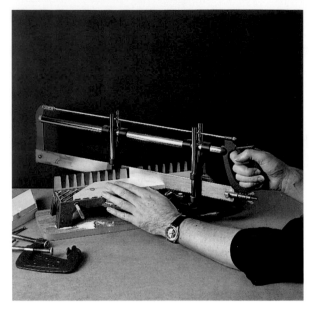

1 Cutting the Wood
Set the miter saw to an angle of 45 degrees and cut out four pieces of wood, two long and two short, angled at each end, to form the four sides of your picture frame.

4 Painting the Frame
Paint the frame with two coats of Antique White, allowing each one to dry thoroughly. Then, draw on wide, equally spaced, stripes in pencil and paint alternate stripes in Provence Blue.

2 Drilling Holes

Rest the frame pieces against a scrap piece of wood to keep them steady. Close to the outside edge of the frame, drill regular holes at ½ in intervals using an electric drill and a ¼ in drill bit.

3 Gluing the Frame

Carefully glue together the four pieces of the frame with wood glue, ensuring that the frame is kept square – we placed ours between two wooden battens. Leave to dry overnight. Fill any gaps with wood filler.

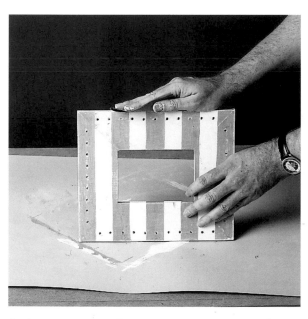

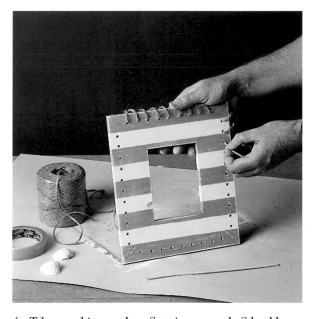

5 Ageing the Frame

Gently sand back with medium-grade sandpaper to age the paintwork. If desired, you can seal the wood with satin varnish or wax if it is to be hung in a wet environment such as a kitchen or a bathroom.

6 Threading the String and Shells

Thread the jute string through the holes and leave two long ends in one corner. Carefully drill holes in the cockleshells using a small ³⁄₁₆ in drill bit. Thread the shells onto the string and allow them to hang down.

This treatment works well on thick, square frames where the paint effect becomes a decorative feature in its own right.

Materials and Tools

Planed pine pre-cut as follows:

4 x: 11 x 3½ x ¾ in

Medium woodstain

Two soft cloths

Water-based paint, Providence Blue and
  Antique White

½ in paintbrush

Overleaf Several woodwork projects, including a peg rail, a picture frame and a bathroom cabinet are gathered together in a seaside bathroom. A pebble border at dado level provides a neat counterpoint to the collection.

1 Staining and Painting

First stain the frame with medium woodstain then apply a coat of water-based Providence Blue paint and allow to dry for 30 minutes. Paint on a blue colorwash diluted in a ratio of 50:50 paint and water.

2 Creating a Limed Effect

When the wash is dry, use Antique White paint to create a fake limed effect. Simply wipe on the paint with one soft, damp cloth and then wipe it back immediately with another. Leave to dry.

3 Limed and Washed

A combination of liming and colorwashing enhances the natural grain of the wood and makes a pleasing, timeworn frame for small images. Wrapped with jute string it becomes a decorative object in its own right.

Our milky sheen technique is perfect for surfaces on which you want a smooth, warm finish to frame your image.

Materials and Tools

Planed pine pre-cut as follows:
4 x: 8 x 2¾ x ¾ in
Water-based paint, Buttermilk and
  Providence Blue
½ in paintbrush
Artists' brush
Kitchen scouring pad
Soft cloth

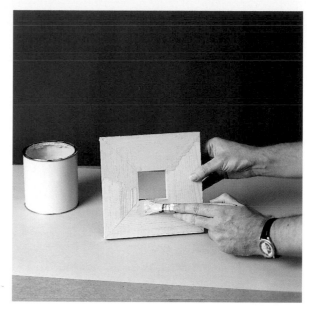

1 Applying the Base Coat
Once you have stuck your frame together with wood glue (see page 43), paint it with one or two coats of the base color, Buttermilk. Allow to dry thoroughly between each application.

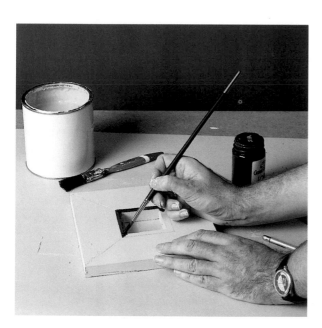

2 Painting the Inner Border
Use an artists' brush to paint a thin border around the frame's aperture in Providence Blue. Choose a color which will enhance the image that you are going to frame and adjust the width of the border accordingly.

3 Creating a Milky Sheen
Gently rub a kitchen scouring pad over the whole frame to create a milky hue. Buff up to a sheen with a soft cloth. Apply a coat of satin varnish or lacquer if the frame is to hang in a kitchen or a bathroom.

This handy little cupboard is another example of one-color ageing and has been embellished with punched tin.

To help keep your work in place while nailing and gluing, don't forget to nail two battens to your worksurface either side of your object. They really do help.

Materials and Tools

Planed pine pre-cut as follows:
2 x: 6 x 2 x ½ in
2 x: 7 x 2 x 1½ in
2 x: *10 x 2 x ½ in
2 x: *8½ x 2 x ½ in
*(cut to a 45 degree angle at one end as
   shown)
3 x: 7 x ¾ x 1½ in
MDF: 6 x 5 x ½ in
Scrap wood for anchoring pieces to
   worksurface
Water-based wood stain, medium
Water-based paint, Antique White
Two small hinges and screws
½ in brads
All-purpose household glue

Small piece of tin	Medium-grade
Short length of rope	sandpaper
Jute string	2in paintbrush
Miter saw	Cotton protective
Electric drill	gloves
¼ in drill bit	Masking tape
Hammer	Awl
Pencil	Wire cutters
Center punch	

1 Assembling the Pieces

Assemble your pieces of pre-cut wood together on a worksurface. Check that they are the right size and arranged in the right configuration. Use a miter saw to create a 45 degree angle on the 4 back pieces.

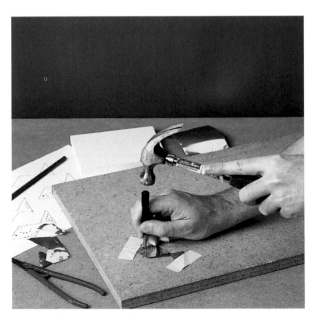

4 Making the Tin Fish

Cut out tin fish using template and wire cutters. The tin is sharp, so wear cotton gloves. Use masking tape to secure fish to a flat piece of wood and use a center punch to create indentations on the back of the fish.

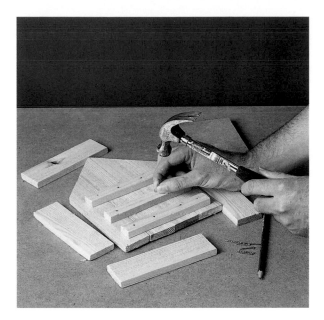

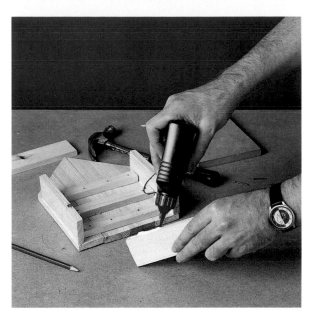

2 Securing the Back

Butt together 4 strips to form the back of the cupboard. Nail on the 3 horizontal battens using brads to secure the back slats. Make sure you allow clearance at the bottom and sides for the walls of the cupboard.

3 Fixing the Walls

Carefully glue the walls in place, by hand or with a glue gun. Attach the side walls first. You'll find that the thickness of the wood and the battens will help you with the positioning. Allow to dry for 24 hours.

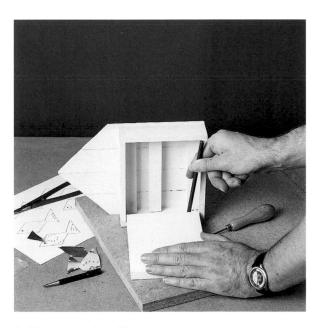

5 Fixing the Door

Stain and paint cupboard and door with medium wood stain. Allow to dry, then apply two coats of Antique White paint. When dry, position and fix the hinges inside the cupboard using an awl and screws.

6 Finishing Touches

Gently sand back cupboard edges to "distress" the paintwork. Glue the tin fish to the front of the door and drill two holes to thread the rope through. Knot in position. Drill another hole for a string door handle.

Ship Ahoy! What bathroom is complete without the ubiquitous driftwood Ocean Liner? In this instance you don't have to scour the local antiques shop to find your weathered piece. You can make it yourself and age it beautifully with a combination of our paint techniques. For a finishing touch we added a small tin anchor. You could also add a nameplate.

Materials and Tools

For the hull:
Sawn pine pre-cut as follows:
1 x: 15 x 4 x 2in sawn pine cut to size

For the decks:
Planed pine pre-cut as follows:
1 x: 10 x 2 x ½ in
1 x: 6 x 2 x ½ in
1 x: 5 x 1 x ½ in

For the mast and funnels:
3 x: ½ in diameter wooden doweling, approximately 2in long, cut to an angle of 30 degrees on a miter saw
2 wooden skewers (or similar)
Water-based paint in 3-4 colors
Latex-based household glue

Thin cardboard	Wire brush
Satin varnish	Hammer
Electric jigsaw	Awl
Miter saw	1 ¼ in brads
Electric drill and ½ in drill bit	Medium-grade sandpaper
Blow torch	

1 Cutting the Pieces
Use a template and jigsaw to cut out a hull shape, including curves. Drill two holes, each ¾ in deep and ½ in wide in the center of the back of the wood to enable you to hang the boat on a wall.

4 Sanding Back
Gently sand back all the paint with medium-grade sandpaper to reveal the base coat and wood. This will give you a pleasant aged appearance. Next, apply a coat of satin varnish.

2 Assembling the Pieces

Take the hull and all the deck pieces and raise the grain on all the pieces which will be visible (see page 14 for instructions). Nail the decks to the hull using brads and a hammer.

3 Painting the Liner

Paint all pieces and masts with two coats of Antique White paint. When dry, paint lower half of hull in New England Red. Leave a white strip, then paint top half of hull. Paint portholes and defining lines.

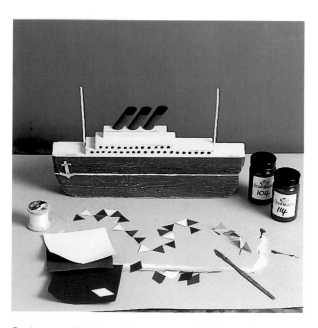

5 Assembling Masts and Bunting

Make two small holes for the wooden skewers and glue in place. For bunting, cut out diamond-shapes in thin cardboard. Paint shapes, then fold them over a thin piece of sewing thread and glue in position.

6 Hanging the Bunting

Hammer in a brad at each end of the hull but leave ½ in protruding. Make a slit at the end of each mast and rest bunting in groove. Wind ends of thread around brads and discard extra bunting.

Walls and Floors

There is life beyond flat latex and that is what this chapter is all about. Creating texture with paper and paint and turning what you thought was an eyesore into an object of desire.

Be assured though that a little faith will allow you to discover that simple color washes are fun, painting stripes and checks a doddle, and that papier mâché is the hottest decorating idea of the decade.

So throw caution to the wind, along with your floor sander and mask, and get ready to conjure up all manner of colored surfaces. A concrete floor can become an asset, corrugated cardboard makes a wonderful dado decoration and old, unwieldy floorboards will disappear before your eyes. For this is paper magic of a different kind – fakery *par excellence*.

Paving the Way

In this chapter we explore two techniques for floors that have hitherto been a nightmare to achieve. We create a Faux Stone Floor (page 62) by using a series of raw umber washes — a veritable *trompe-l'oeil* if ever there was one, but without the trauma. From more Northern climes, a checkered floor (page 60) which can lend even the worst surfaces an air of understated elegance.

For the walls, it gets even easier. Beige and white paint form the basis of a faded plaster wall, a fresco border highlights and underscores perfectly your favorite *objets trouvés* (page 70) and, amazingly, it takes just a few minutes to achieve. There's a simple wallwash (page 68) that will create the translucent delicacy of watercolors and finally, some classic Gustavian stripes (page 65), as you've never seen them before. Inspired by French châteaux, the *pièce de résistance* for us is the papier mâché frieze (page 74) using only recycled cardboard, newspaper and electrical cording, it brings 3-D relief to any wall. Say goodbye to plaster and a big hello to pulp. From now on, there will be a new meaning to washing the floors and walls.

Our new-generation, specialist water-based paint is ideal for use on walls. Its chalky texture has fresco-like qualities and for flat work, you can use the paint straight from the can. The only word of caution is that for large areas of dark color you should apply a top coat of water-based lacquer or satin varnish to prevent marks showing on the surface.

But it is this very chalky texture that to our mind renders the paint perfect for colorwashing walls. There's no need to dilute it into ten different strengths and then painstakingly apply each coat. One or two washes, painted on top of a pale background, will suffice. Most of the rough edges or brushmarks can be wiped away with a cloth when applying the wash. But more importantly, a light, gentle sanding at the end of the process will result in a delightfully muted appearance. As with all paint, coverage will depend on the porosity of your walls. In their natural state, that is, undiluted, the paints are designed to be applied generously and not "spread" like latex — rollers are fine for flat work.

Opposite Broken color, achieved by means of a colorwash using diluted water-based paint, is equally effective on flat or textured walls.

Floors

Preparing Floors

To a degree, the amount of preparation necessary for a painted floor is determined by the condition of the floor and by how much of a perfectionist you are. In our world, the whole point of the exercise is to disguise a less-than-perfect floor, with as little effort as possible.

Obviously if you have huge holes, protruding nails or floorboards that see-saw when you tread on them, these need attention, as do left-over pieces of linoleum. Consider using expanding spray foam as filler for large holes, or kitchen and bathroom sealant to block off any drafts.

If your floorboards are waxy and greasy, use a furniture cleaner especially designed to remove wax and some steel wool to clean them up, or try a good wash with sugar soap and a stout brush. Neither are as bad as they sound. Leave your clean floor overnight to dry completely, then seal it all over with diluted white household glue, mixed one-to-one with water.

If you are using regular latex paint, apply a coat of acrylic wood primer before painting. If you are using water-based paints, simply apply two coats of your chosen base color.

Concrete floors need to be sound and free from damp. Again, you should fill any gaping holes. Apart from that, you can go straight ahead and seal the surface with a diluted wash of white household glue, as for floorboards.

Marking Out the Design

The simpler your floor design, the more effective and successful it is likely to be. The classic checkered floor never tires with age. Don't be alarmed at the thought of marking out your design. With a little planning and the knowledge that from on high the eye is easily deceived, you really can afford to feel confident.

For a simple checkered floor cut out an accurate square template using thick card. A set square and ruler will ensure complete accuracy. Establish a central line down the middle of the room by measuring the center point between the opposite side walls at each end of the room. Join up these points using a long straight wooden batten and chinagraph pencil or by snapping a chalk line on it.

Put two of the opposing points of the square diamond-like on to the central line and create your first square. Using the batten, carefully extend one of the diagonals in each direction – this is the most important line, so try to be accurate. Then, by placing your template at each end of your newly created diagonal line, you can mark where a parallel line should go. Repeat the process for the opposite diagonal and you can see how easily you can build-up the squares in each direction, using your set square and template to keep you in line.

More complicated patterns should be worked out first to scale on a piece of paper. And if you are blessed with an oddly shaped room, a simple border around the design could help to seal in the pattern visually.

Opposite A simple checkered pattern in two colors will disguise a less than perfect floor and is much cheaper than carpeting. When you tire of it, you can easily change the color or the design, or both. See overleaf for step-by-step instructions.

Checkered Floor

There's no doubt about it, there is something distinctly Swedish about our grey and white checkered floor, yet it is another fine example of "Fabulous Faux".

This painted, patterned floor is quite charming, almost dainty, but sophisticated too. It is highly durable and our treatment covers up the worst of all possible surfaces – an unsightly combination of concrete and floorboards.

The joy of this technique is that you do not have to be precisely accurate when painting the squares, and the final coating of varnish gives a hardwearing and distinctly elegant finish.

You can use regular latex paint for these floors, in which case you should use a primer first, but we used our own water-based paint. For preparing and marking out floors for painting, see page 58.

Materials and Tools

Water-based paint, or regular latex in two
  different colors. We used Antique White
  and Elephant Grey
Water-based floor varnish
White household glue diluted 1:1 with
  water
One large (4in) and one small
  (1in) paintbrush
Two soft cloths
Long wooden straightedge
Pencil
Set square

1 Preparing and Sealing
Prepare floorboards as described on page 58. Seal the floor with a thinned-down coat of glue (1:1). Leave to dry for several hours then apply two coats of Antique White paint.

4 Ageing the Grey
Thin some Antique White paint with water, at least three parts water to one part paint. Wash the solution lightly over the grey squares using a soft cloth, then mop up any excess with a second dry cloth.

2 Marking out Squares

Use the wood, set square and pencil to mark out a grid-like pattern across the floor, creating 20in diamonds with a template. Start at one corner. As long as the first square is exact, you can run a grid from it.

3 Painting the Squares

Paint alternate squares in Elephant Grey. It is not as difficult as you might think, especially as any blemishes or small lines tend to disappear when the floor is viewed from on high and when furniture is in place.

5 Sealing and Finishing

Brush the whole floor with three coats of the water-based varnish, allowing each coat to dry thoroughly (it should be touch-dry within 30 minutes). It will be milky at first, but dries to a flat sheen.

6 The Finished Floor

These painted floorboards with their slightly aged and delicately colored checkerboard design disguise a less than perfect surface. The ideal solution for wooden floors, or indeed concrete or hardboard.

Faux Stone Floor

Our Faux Stone Floor offers the perfect way to liven up a concrete surface. It is really an exercise in using raw umber, or "instant ageing in a tube" as we call it. It is, in fact, an artists' paint which can be diluted to different strengths for quick, easy and very effective decorating. We have watched customers raking their heels over our shop's painted concrete floor, in disbelief, once they realize that the flagstones are not real.

Raw umber can be used in a variety of ways, but this project calls for an acrylic version, diluted with water to form a liquid mud. You will need to apply two or three washes of variously diluted raw umber, each of which is a very runny paint of ever-increasing color strength. When applied, then ragged off (mopped-up) with a soft, dry cloth, the paint will leave patches of shadow that create realistic-looking flagstones before your very eyes.

Materials and Tools

White household glue diluted 1:1 with
   water
Water-based exterior paint (smooth finish),
   beige
A darker beige-grey water-based paint for
   the grout (latex is fine)
Water-based floor varnish, satin
Acrylic raw umber
Large 6in, medium 2in and small ½in paint
   brushes
Tape measure/set square
Long piece of scrap wood for drawing
   straight edges
Two soft cloths

1 Sealing and Painting
Once the floor is clean and dry, seal it with a thinned down coat of glue (1:1). Leave to dry for several hours. Apply one or two coats of beige exterior paint. Allow to dry for a minimum of 4 hours.

4 Applying the Grout
When the flagstones are dry, after 30 minutes, paint in the "grout" with a strong coat (1in paint to 3.5 fl oz water) of the darker beige, with a small, ½in brush.

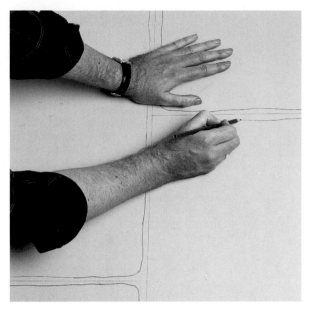

2 Marking Out the Flagstones

Mark out horizontal lines, 24 in apart. Add vertical lines to create square boxes. We staggered the boxes, like brickwork. Draw in rounded "flagstones" freehand, leaving sufficent room for the "grout".

3 Ageing the Surface

With a weak raw umber solution (1in paint to 7 fl oz water), apply "shadows" and rag-off harsh edges to create "dimples". Repeat with stronger solution (1in paint to 3.5 fl oz water).

5 Raw Umber Finish

When the "grout" is dry, after about 30 minutes, paint on some of the stronger raw umber wash again and leave to dry (no need to rag-off this time).This will lend extra depth and texture to the floor.

6 Finishing Off

For a tough and durable shine, brush on three coats of the floor varnish. Allow each coat to dry thoroughly (touch-dry after 30 minutes). It will appear milky when first applied but will clear as it dries.

Gustavian Stripes

Some classics are hard to beat. We've given this project a deliberate Nordic touch since Scandinavia boasts a unique position in the world of design – where else does ancient tradition co-exist with the clean lines of modern innovation so spectacularly?

The same is true of our stripes. The result can be as traditional or as contemporary as you wish. Color is the determining factor. You can see clearly the faded grandeur here, beautifully enhanced with the rich symmetry of candlelight. But imagine the freshness and verve you could create by using Lime Green or Provence Blue paint instead. Raw umber artists' paint applied over the white color also helps to create a well-worn look.

Painting stripes is not as tricky as it first appears. It is a lot easier than hanging striped wallpaper that's for sure. And you'll find the eye is blissfully forgiving when taking in only the whole picture. It tends not to home in on any wobbly lines or deviations that you might have unwittingly introduced. Stripes may be a well-used classic but they are one of our all-time favorite motifs.

Materials and Tools

Water-based paint, (matte latex would be
    fine too) Antique White and Stockholm
    Blue
Pencil
Spirit level
Wooden batten, approximately 5½ in wide
4 in paintbrush
Piece of card
Fine-grade sandpaper
Wallpaper paste brush
Soft cloth

1 Base Coat and Stripes
Paint the wall with a flat coat of Antique White paint.
Use a spirit level and wooden batten to accurately
mark 5½ in-wide stripes. Allow double the width, 11 in,
between each stripe.

2 Painting on the Stripes
Apply one coat of water-based Stockholm Blue paint to
the stripes using a wallpaper paste brush. Try to keep
the edges neat and clean but don't worry too much as
small mistakes will not show.

3 Masking and Sanding Back
Use a piece of card to mask off the white background
as you lightly sand each stripe. This sanding breaks the
surface of the paint and creates rich textures and tones
in the color.

Wallwash and Border

While we have irreverently named this project "Santorini Wash and Brush Up", our inspiration came from two other geographical sources; the faded walls of a fisherman's cottage in France and the glaze on some beautiful Italian ceramic pots we discovered by chance in London.

Color-washing is nothing more than a series of variously watered-down paints, layered one on top of another over a related, pale base coat. For true color-washing, you always start with the weakest solution first and build up the color slowly. We've taken a short cut here by using just one wash, then toning it down with a top wash of Antique White. Always test a small area before you start.

For a wet environment such as a kitchen or bathroom, apply a coat of water-based satin varnish to protect the surface from moisture.

Materials and Tools

Water-based paint, Caribbean Green and
  Antique White, both diluted 1 part paint to
  4-5 parts water
Pale blue paint for base
  (latex is fine)
Water-based paint, Provence Blue and
  Stockholm Blue
Spirit level
Pencil
Fine-grade sandpaper
Wallpaper paste brush
Artists' brush
Two soft cloths

1 Base Coat and Border
Apply a flat coat of pale blue paint and allow to dry. Use a spirit level to draw two horizontal pencil lines across the wall, creating a thin stripe. Paint in between the lines with Provence Blue. Sand back.

2 Applying the First Wash
When the painted stripe is completely dry, paint on the diluted Caribbean Green with an artists' brush, allowing areas of the base color to show through. Work on a small area at a time.

3 Avoiding Paint Drips
Catch any drips or runs with a soft cloth and continue to rub-in the wash to the wall with a second cloth. Avoid any obvious swirly patterns which would detract from the gentle, all-over wash.

4 Applying the Second Wash
In a similar manner, paint on the diluted Antique White paint, (1 part paint to 4-5 parts water), ragging off as before to avoid any drips. Rub-in the wash using a soft cloth and working a small area at a time.

5 Making the Second Stripe
Use a pencil and spirit level to draw on a thicker stripe above the first one. Vary the thickness of your stripe according to the proportions of your wall. Paint the stripe with Stockholm Blue. Allow to dry.

6 Sanding and Finishing
Give the entire wall a light sanding with fine-grade sandpaper to soften the edges of the stripes. Concentrate on the borders, rubbing them back as far as desired. Wipe away with a dry cloth.

Faded Fresco Border

Have you ever peeled back layers of wall-paper to reveal a beaten-up plaster wall which you actually quite like? Well, here's a contemporary version that simulates a muted, gently aged wall but is rather more practical to create and easy to live with.

Materials and Tools

Medium-grade sandpaper

Water-based paint, Olive Green

Flat matte white paint for the base (latex is fine)

4in paintbrush

Pencil

Spirit level

1 Tracing the Border

Mark the exact shape of the mirror and create a 6in border in pencil around this. Leave a ½in gap between the edge of the mirror and border for added definition.

2 Applying the Border Color

Use a 4in brush to apply a fairly light, single coat of Olive Green paint. Take care not to paint over the lines too much unless you want an irregular edge on your border.

3 Sanding the Border

Use medium-grade sandpaper to lightly sand the whole border then concentrate more on random areas to reveal patches of color beneath. Experiment until you have achieved your desired effect.

Distressed Plaster Wall

The perfect backdrop for our papier mâché frieze, this distressed plaster wall effect does away with the need for layer upon layer of colorwashing. We simply used two washes and some "dabbing" to create a textured, irregular finish.

Materials and Tools

Water-based paint, Antique White
  and Beige
Wallpaper paste brush
Three soft cloths
Fine-grade sandpaper

1 Applying the First Wash
First paint the walls in a flat coat of Antique White. Leave to dry for an hour or so then apply a wash of Beige paint, diluted to at least 1:1 water and paint. Work on a small area at a time.

2 Ragging Off
Mop up any runs of paint you create with a soft cloth and rub-in the wash with another cloth working a small area at a time again. Avoid creating any swirly patterns which will detract from the fresco effect.

3 Applying Texture and Sanding
When whole area is "washed", dab on haphazard strokes of Antique White, leaving small, irregular areas of Beige showing through. Gently sand back to soften edges. Wipe away dust with soft, dry cloth.

Papier Mâché Frieze

As a prelude to the following chapter, Paper Magic, here's an idea that we hope will really inspire you. To be honest, we think it's one of our best ...

In the interiors of crumbling French châteaux or rambling Italian farmhouses, you'll often find that plaster friezes have been added to large, flat walls to create interest or to divide and separate certain areas – anything from a simple dado rail to something rather more elaborate.

Closer to home, it has to be said that even in the most humble abode there are times when a flat wall is just not good enough. There are times, frankly, when a little 3-D relief is what is required.

Now, using little more than some recycled corrugated cardboard boxes and newspaper, you can create a stylish frieze that will add scenic interest to any room. It's a technique that can be applied to virtually any design – and with practice and a little patience, we're convinced you can emulate the grand friezes of times gone by. See previous page for the finished frieze.

Materials and Tools

Newspaper strips	Craft knife
Latex-based household glue	1 in paintbrush
	Steel rule
Acrylic gesso	Spirit level
Acrylic raw umber	Pencil
Water-based paint,	Soft cloth
Beige (optional) and Antique White	

1 Cutting the Squares
Using a craft knife and a steel rule, cut out sufficient identical 3in cardboard squares and ¾in deep border stripes, also cardboard, to cover the required area twice over.

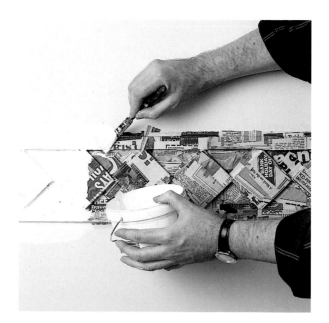

4 Coating with Gesso
Leave to dry for at least 24 hours. Once the wall is completely dry, apply 3-4 coats of gesso, allowing each one to dry thoroughly. Unsightly ridges can be given a light sanding.

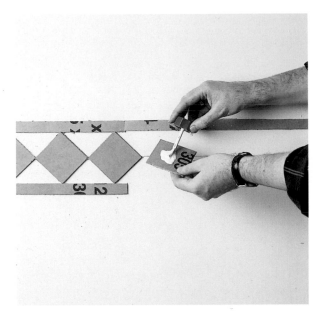

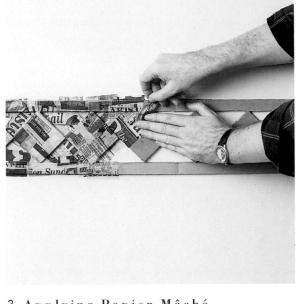

2 Attaching the Border

Use a spirit level to draw a horizontal guide line at the required height on your wall. Glue the strips and squares to the wall with latex glue. When dry, glue another layer directly on top for extra depth.

3 Applying Papier Mâché

Glue on newspaper strips over the cardboard cut-outs. Apply two layers of newspaper and ensure that the top and bottom run of paper protrude by about ¼ in up the wall.

5 Further Ageing

Use a paintbrush to gently apply a light coat of raw umber to the white stripes. Wipe away any drips with a soft cloth. For a faded plaster look, apply a coat of water-based Beige paint.

6 Distressing the Surface

Quickly paint on a light wash of diluted water-based Antique White paint (at least 1:1 paint to water), and then apply solid Antique White with a dry paintbrush. Leave to dry.

Paper Magic

For most of us, the term "papier mâché" evokes dim memories of the schoolroom. Even now, given that the craft has been elevated to a fresh and exciting art form, the basic ingredients can still end up as a rather sad piece.

Most papier mâché *objets*, despite looking beautiful can, on closer inspection, appear flimsy or lightweight. Undoubtedly, the most successful pieces have endured layer upon layer of paper, which, frankly, few of us have the time or inclination to accomplish.

What we've tried to do is to provide some catalysts, adding extra components that assist the process, yet keeping the spirit and not harming the end result. Something from nothing hits new heights as we add such items as electrical cording, string and card to the traditional recipe. We call it Paper Engineering.

Paper Techniques

Somewhat surprisingly, in the late 18th and 19th centuries, papier mâché was used to create architectural moldings – anything from ceiling roses to bulkheads and panels in steamboats and railway carriages of the day. The "pulp" method was by far the most common, yet layering on a grand scale was available at the very top end of the market – where large panels were made of anything up to 120 layers of paper!

You could say that our Frieze (page 74) is a distant relation of the ancient technique. The aim is the same, but the end result is a great deal easier to achieve. Papier mâché pulp is, quite literally, mashed paper – a malleable pulp that can be molded into shape and then left to dry. It is certainly less labor-intensive than the layering method, but is altogether more organic in appearance. This kind of pulp looks rather like an eggbox, and to our minds, is an acquired taste.

The basic method requires soaking small, torn pieces of newspaper in water for 24 hours. The paper can then be placed, bit by bit, into a blender with some more water and whizzed until you have a wet, pulp mixture. This is then sieved and drained to extract all the liquid. Finally, white household glue is added until the pulp feels like soft clay.

The advantage with this method is that the pulp is now ready to be molded into your desired object. Different colors and textures can be achieved by using different papers.

However, if this all sounds a bit fussy, and images of a clogged up blender loom large, then a much better option is to buy the ready-made commercial equivalent, modeling material (see page 82).

The method of papier mâché layering is of course a classic – torn strips of newspaper are layered with a glue. This can be flour and water mixed together or, more practically, a wallpaper paste.

To prevent the possibility of mold, your work must be allowed to dry after every one or two layers of newspaper have been applied. Once again, different textures can be achieved by using different papers. Tissue paper is especially good for fixing over chicken-wire frameworks, as it dries to a tight skin. Sugar paper leaves a more textured finish.

Almost any 3-D papier mâché project will require a mold. Our additives become a deliberate and integral part of the design, but if you are using existing jugs or bowls, make sure you use a masking agent such as petroleum jelly or plastic wrap, otherwise your prized jug will unwittingly become integrated as well!

Our Noah's Ark Frieze (page 86) is just perfect for a child's room — it's educational and, if you're brave enough, is a project which they could join in with too! (see the special note about wallpaper paste first though).

If you survive that experience, you can move on to the Pulp Sculpture Plaque (Page 83) — a sure testament to the fact that graphics do have an exciting, fun role to play in modern decoration. Aside from the examples we've shown, the possibilities are endless — imagine a library with the letters of the alphabet "cast" around the room, or a simple leaf motif placed around a door or used as a frame for a mirror above a fireplace.

We also show you how, with a little imagination, a few boards nailed together and embellished with ready-made pulp and just two layers of papier mâché, can lead to masterful results.

You'll also be delighted to hear that there's very little chance of repetitive strain injury if you follow our way to create the classic Papier Mâché Bowl (page 80). With the addition of some sturdy legs made from modeling material and a robust rim, the bowl looks and feels substantial.

Lastly, we use the same embellishments to transform standard gift boxes into little treasures. Pulp non-fiction at its finest … For more inspiration, take a look at the work of Julie Arkell, Marion Elliot or Deborah Schneebeli-Morrell, who have created beautiful pieces along these lines, including jewellery and dolls' houses.

Papier Mâché Bowl

Papier mâché objects as art forms can sometimes feel distinctly flimsy unless you use many, many layers of newspaper. We managed to overcome this problem with the papier mâché frieze and pulp sculpture plaque on pages 73 and 83, by creating mass with materials other than newspaper. Similarly, we have transformed the ubiquitous papier mâché bowl by using other "additives". The end result is robust, sturdy and above all good to look at.

Materials and Tools

Newspaper strips	Three-core electrical
Wallpaper paste	cording
Acrylic-based gesso	Gilding paste
Modeling material	Water-based paint
Latex-based	Double-sided tape
household glue	Bucket or container
Masking tape	to hold balloon
½ in wide jute string	Scalpel

1 Making the Bowl Mold
Blow up a balloon to the required size and rest it in a container that allows a bowl shape to be visible. Use masking tape to hold the balloon in place. Paste on one layer of newspaper strips and allow to dry.

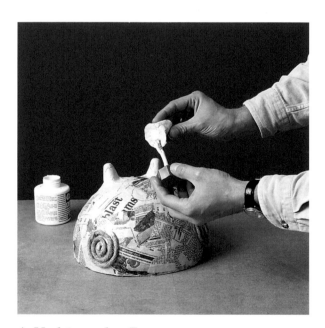

4 Making the Feet
For the feet, use modeling material cut into three. Press against the bowl and fix with latex-based household glue and masking tape. Then apply two layers of papier mâché, allowing each to dry.

2 Layering the Bowl

Following the technique on page 78, apply 10 layers of newspaper over several days, allowing each layer to dry. When the bowl shape is completely dry, use a craft knife to remove the bowl, and burst the balloon.

3 Applying String Embellishment

Wind the jute string into a spiral and bind both ends with masking tape. Place the spiral onto double-side tape, remove the protective paper and stick the taped-coil to the bowl.

5 Creating the Rim

To make the rim, carefully slice open the electrical cord with a scalpel and remove the wires. Use the remaining shell to loop over the bowl rim. Papier mâché in place with two layers and allow to dry.

6 Finishing Off

Paint the bowl with two or three coats of gesso, then apply your colors. We used Pumpkin for the inside, followed by Cornflower Blue for the outer edges. Enhance the spirals and rim with gold gilding paste.

Pulp Sculpture Fireplace

As every devotee of papier mâché knows, there are two basic methods you can follow. One involves strips of newspaper applied with a wallpaper paste. The other, more laborious, technique calls for "cooking" newspaper to a pulp. Thankfully you can buy a ready-made modeling material that perfectly emulates papier mâché pulp. It is better to allow the modeling material to harden before covering it with papier mâché, but not absolutely necessary.

Pulp sculpture has the same enormous potential offered by conventional papier mâché; you use it in exactly the same way to create 3-D relief. Here we've nailed together a few planks of wood to create a fireplace, then embellished it with modeling material and papier mâché to create a simple floral design that becomes gloriously rich when burnished with gold and raw umber. See overleaf for instructions on how to make our 3-D plaque.

Materials and Tools

Modeling material	Rolling pin
Latex-based	Craft knife
household glue	Medium-grade
Newspaper strips	sandpaper
Wallpaper paste	A soft, clean cloth
Acrylic gesso	Stippling brush
Acrylic raw umber	Wooden board
Gilding paste	

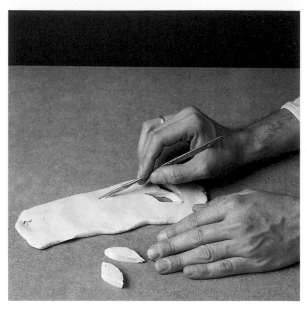

1 Cutting Out Leaf Shapes
Roll out the modeling material with a rolling pin and cut leaf shapes freehand with a craft knife. Roll a small chunk of modeling material into an oval ball shape and flatten the back directly onto a fireplace.

2 Attaching the Shapes
Glue the shapes into position and cover with two layers of papier mâché. When papier mâché is dry, sand the edges and apply 3 coats of gesso, allowing each to dry. Age with raw umber and gilding paste.

Pulp Sculpture Plaque

There is definitely life beyond the dado rail you know. Well, at least there is if you let your imagination move one step on from our papier mâché frieze concept (see page 73) into the world of paper sculpture.

Don't be alarmed. In our terms, pulp sculpture is nothing more than adding even more texture to a surface by placing a variety of materials between the surface and the papier mâché. You're creating form by using posterboard, electrical cording, string, rope and modeling material.

We've used the technique to create our very own plaque, as a permanent reminder that 1987 was the year in which our first shop opened (see page 83). You may wish to record another special date — the age of your house for example, a family name, or a more abstract design.

Materials and Tools

¼ in posterboard (available from most
   Art Stores)
Jute string
3-core electrical cording
Latex-based household glue
Newspaper strips
Wallpaper paste
Water-based paint, Antique White
Acrylic gesso
Acrylic raw umber
Gilding paste
Push pins
Hammer and nails
Pencil
Medium-grade sandpaper
Artists' brush
Stippling brush

1 Making the Oval
To cut and draw an oval frame from the posterboard, place two push pins or nails down the center of the board. Surround them with a loop of string and trace an oval with an upright pencil.

4 Applying Papier Mâché and Gesso
Now papier mâché the entire design with two layers of newspaper (see page 78 for technique). Allow to dry and apply at least 3 coats of gesso. Sand back rough edges. Apply two coats of Antique White paint.

2 Applying the Decoration

Decide on your form of decoration, then cut out posterboard shapes accordingly. Glue them to the wall. If you are using letters, space them correctly on a piece of paper, then trace over them and transfer to wall.

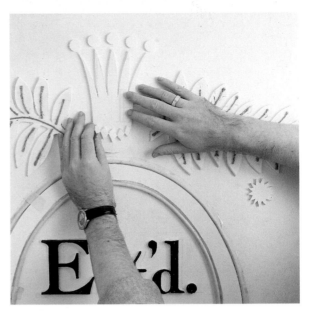

3 Embellishing the Design

To create even more relief or texture, embellish the posterboard shapes with other materials. We have used string for leaf veins and stripped electrical cording for an effective rounded oval border.

5 Ageing the Surface

Apply a lightly diluted wash of raw umber (a 2 in smear of paint to 7 fl oz water). Make sure that the wash is applied to all the crevices. Use a soft cloth to mop up drips and smooth edges.

6 Applying the Highlights

Use a stippling brush for applying gilding paste to form gold highlights. For small edges, apply the paste with your finger. The end result is an elegant, subtly faded plaque to grace any wall.

Noah's Ark

Here's a project (see previous page) that's designed for a children's room or a playroom and one that youngsters can join in with too. If your children do help with this project, please remember that most proprietary brands of wallpaper paste contain fungicide and are therefore unsuitable for child-use. Non-toxic paste powder is available from educational suppliers, craft stores and some specialist decorating suppliers. Using the same theory as the more formal frieze on page 73, the Noah's Ark can be embellished in many different ways. Or the theme could be completely different, such as a three-dimensional dolls' house or a parade of brightly colored shops.

To create "After Noah", photocopy and enlarge the templates at the back of the book to give you the basic animal shapes, or invent your own. Cut out the shapes with a scalpel and use repositionable spray adhesive to mount the animals on the posterboard or thick cardboard. You will find that posterboard is much easier to cut than thick card. Then follow the instructions opposite.

Materials and Tools

¼ in posterboard
Newspaper strips
Wallpaper paste
Acrylic gesso
Latex-based household glue
Water-based paint in several colors
Artists' brush
Stippling brush
Scalpel
Pencil eraser
Tracing paper for stencils

1 Papier Mâché for Animals
Once you have decided on the quantity and style of your animals, cut out posterboard shapes and glue them to the wall. Apply two layers of papier mâché (see page 78) to cover the animals.

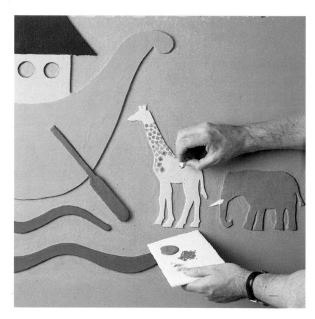

4 Animal Decoration
Cut a square-shaped stamp from a pencil eraser and use it to apply markings to the giraffe using light brown paint. Allow the squares to overlap the edges and use a darker brown paint to create shadows.

2 Applying the Gesso

Leave the papier mâché to dry for 24 hours, then paint on three coats of acrylic gesso using an artists' brush. Allow each coat of gesso to dry for 2-3 hours before applying the next one.

3 Decorating the Animals

Now decorate the animals by hand. Make your own paper stencil using the templates at the back of the book to paint on the stripes of the zebra with a ¾ in stippling brush.

5 Embellishing the Design

Decoration and embellishment are up to you. We added three-dimensional ears and tusks to the elephant, a scroll to the edge of the ark and stippled white paint to the crests of the waves. You could also add shutters to the ark windows, fish to the sea, or more animals protruding from the portholes. This project is creative, educational and fun. It won't take 40 days and 40 nights to make either!

Decorated Boxes

Any idea of making your own papier mâché pulp is by now probably redundant, given that ready-made modeling material is such a joy to use. As in previous projects, the finishing touch is a final coating of acrylic gesso – four coats are best. The gesso acts as a thick primer, sealing in the porous newspaper to leave a solid white chalky surface – perfect for further embellishment.

Materials and Tools

Various-sized boxes	Gilding paste
Modeling material	Rolling pin
Newspaper strips	Pastry cutters
Latex-based	Palette knife
household glue	½ in paintbrush
Acrylic gesso	Soft cloth

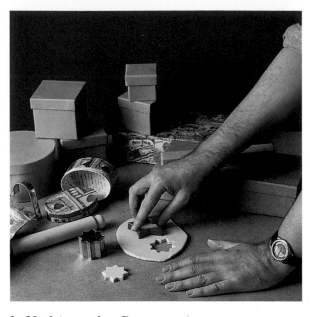

1 Making the Decorations
Roll out the modeling material until it is about ¼ in thick. Use pastry cutters or a palette knife to create a variety of shapes. Leave them to dry for an hour then glue them to a box.

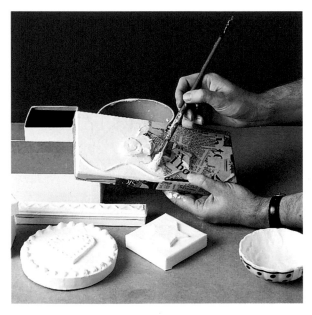

2 Applying Papier Mâché
Cover the decoration with two layers of papier mâché then leave to dry thoroughly (24 hours minimum). Coat the whole box with 2-3 coats of gesso, allowing each coat to dry before applying the next.

3 Gold Embellishments
Using the tip of your finger or a paintbrush, gently highlight the raised areas with the gilding paste. Allow to dry and rub to a shine with a soft cloth. For another finishing touch, line the box with decorative paper.

Applied Art

Who was it that said "the sum of two parts is greater than the whole"? Whoever it was, they must have had Chapter Five of this book in mind when they said it. For it is here that we endeavor to produce a final flourish to decorated surfaces by adding some fairly mundane ingredients, such as pebbles or string. It is here that unloved china becomes mosaic and that a discarded cabinet is completely rejuvenated with a tin panel.

Otherwise known as the glorious art of "sticking-it-on", Applied Art allows your imagination to run riot as you gather together all manner of household items in order to adorn and restore those pieces of furniture or decorative objects whose glory has long faded.

Cut and Paste

We have created here a positively eclectic mix of ideas whose origins span the globe but enjoy a common theme. It's all about texture again, mixing materials that work in harmony with one another. And it's the perfect opportunity to bring wit to your décor. Here are a few of the materials we have used to create our projects. There are many others that would be equally suitable.

Tin

The folk art of Mexico and India and the Shaker movement are the influences for our Punched Tin Cupboard (page 96). Truly there's no better example of the theory behind this chapter than our cupboard. What was once sad and delapidated now has style and a quirky charm all of its own, thanks to a little help from some tin, a pot of glue and, of course, paint.

Tin is fun to use and looks extremely stylish when combined with wood. We show you how to embellish a simple wooden picture frame with a punched tin design that really lends charm to the finished piece. A great idea would be to carefully cut some naïve shapes like a bird, a house or a tree from pine or MDF, paint and age them in New England Red or Providence Blue, and add small punched tin panels – wonderful Christmas decorations that even the Shakers would approve of – and you can use them year after year. The tin we have used for the projects is sold as galvanized steel sheeting and is inexpensive to buy. See the suppliers list on page 130 for details.

Mosaic

For many, collecting shells from the beach is akin to a national pastime. Shells are wonderfully tactile and endlessly collectable. However, once you've brought them home, what do you do with them? They can easily look like a tacky souvenir. One way of solving this is to use patterns and repeats of the same shell, rather than a haphazard mix, just like the shellwork boxes, frames and urns of 1950s France.

Our Mosaic Pot is a good solution for all your seashell and china paraphernalia. Our pot was inspired by a huge version we saw in the grounds of a beautiful French villa. Thankfully though, our smaller version still manages to evoke the Mediterranean without requiring an investment in French real estate. More importantly, it is quick and easy to do and would work equally well on mirrors, frames, boxes and friezes (see page 102 for our pebble frieze).

The same technique would also be fine for garden tabletops and lampbases. Now that small glass pieces (tesserae) are available commercially, they would be a most suitable alternative.

String

Style magazines often use string or rope to improve decorative items and even larger pieces of furniture too – nautical they may be, but just how practical and comfortable is a chair tied with rope and finished off with a string knot? More sensible and effective then, is our string-covered candlestick and lampshade. This technique is ideal for covering and transforming any lampbase or pot whose shape and color has become dated.

String and rope make excellent tassels or tie-backs and provide a decorative pattern for our String and Calico curtains on page 104. They are instant curtains that are practical, inexpensive and wildly contemporary.

Overleaf Objects embellished with punched tin look completely at home in a garden room, a living room or indeed a kitchen or bathroom.

Punched Tin Cupboard

One of our all-time favorite decorative techniques is punched tin – whether it be the simple tin objects beloved by the Shaker movement or the more elaborate but equally decorative boxes and lanterns of Mexico and India.

Surprisingly, punched tin is not difficult to create, neither does it take too long to do. Yet the finished result is incredibly effective. This design took about an hour to make. By simply gluing a punched tin panel onto an existing door we transformed an old, unwanted cupboard into a highly desirable object.

The key to success is to use a simple design. We chose a motif from a greeting card as a starting point. For a slightly different look we've used "reversed punching" here – that is, the design is punched into, rather than out from, the reverse side of the tin. By using several different-sized punches we were able to create different-sized indents which create added interest and texture.

Punched tin can be used to liven up all sorts of faded treasures. Dispense with découpage and bring on the punch!

Materials and Tools

Tin-plate (galvanized steel sheet)	Pencil
Heavy duty glue or epoxy resin and spreader	Center punch and hammer
Tracing paper	Repositionable spray adhesive
Water-based paint, Forest Green and Terracotta	Steel wool
	Lighter fluid

1 Ageing the Cupboard

Two-color age the cupboard with one or two coats of water-based Forest Green paint over two coats of Terracotta (see page 22 for technique). Sand back and wax according to the two-color ageing technique.

2 Transferring the Design

Use a pencil to draw your design on to tracing paper, then apply a light coating of repositionable spray adhesive to stick the tracing paper face down, on to the back of the tin sheet.

3 Punching the Design

Hammer the center punch into the tin at regular intervals to create indentations. (Practice first on a spare piece of tin). Before removing tracing paper, check that the whole design has transferred to the tin.

4 Attaching the Tin Panel

Glue the tin panel to the cupboard door and leave to dry overnight. Keep the metal flat by weighting it with books or something similar. The next day, remove excess glue with steel wool dampened with lighter fluid.

Punched Tin Picture Frame

Following on from the Punched Tin Cupboard project, the same basic punching techniques can be used to transform a precut piece of MDF (medium-density fiberboard) into a pretty picture frame.

The only part of this project which calls for a high degree of accuracy is the cutting out of the aperture in the frame. The rest is plain sailing. Simple, naïve designs are the easiest to transfer to tin, while clear lettering can also be fun and effective.

Not only are the possibilities of punched tin designs endless, you can also embellish the tin itself with large black tacks or round-topped carpet pins. Or try a series of cut-out shapes — birds, fish, festive angels and trees.

To make life easier, always make your aperture slightly smaller than that of a standard clip-frame. That way, you will be able to attach the glass and backing from the clip frame to your homemade frame, making the final assembly much easier.

Materials and Tools

Tin-plate (galvanized steel sheet)
One piece MDF cut to size, approximately
    12 x 12in
Water-based paint, Forest Green
Tracing paper
Masking tape
½in brass tacks
Center punch and hammer
Electric jigsaw
Protective cotton gloves
Wire cutters
Electric drill and ½in drill bit
Felt pen and pencil

1 Cutting Out the Aperture

Trace out an aperture on to the MDF and drill a ½ in hole within the area. Use an electric jigsaw to gently cut out the aperture. Paint with two coats of Forest Green water-based paint.

2 Cutting Out the Tin

Place the MDF frame on top of the tin and trace around it using a felt pen. Wearing cotton gloves, carefully cut out the tin with wire cutters. It should be about ¼ in smaller than the frame itself.

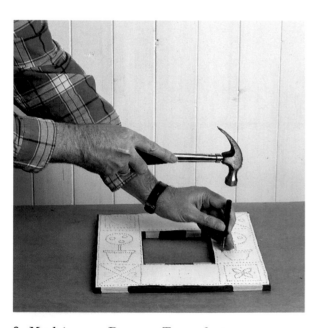

3 Making a Paper Template

Make another template of the MDF frame using tracing paper and stick it to the tin-plate frame with masking tape. Draw on your design using pencil dots, then center punch all the dots around the edges.

4 Punching the Holes

Fix the tin plate to the frame with ½ in brass tacks hammered into the indentations around the edge. Replace the tracing and center punch the rest of your design using a hammer.

Pebble Frieze

We've always liked the modern-day equivalents of naïve Greco-Roman mosaics that are found around ornamental fountains in stylish gardens the world over.

Similarly, pebbles and shells set in grout in a bathroom create a dramatic backdrop, so here's our Pebble Frieze. In a bathroom or kitchen, seal the frieze with satin varnish to protect the paint from moisture.

Materials and Tools

Waterproof ceramic tile adhesive	½ in quadrant molding
Pebbles	Spatula
Water-based paint, Antique White	Glue gun/brads or screws
Spirit level	Artists' brush

1 Fixing and Filling Moldings
Mark a guideline on the wall and glue, nail or screw the moldings in place, approximately 1½ in apart. Fill in two-thirds of the space between the moldings with tile adhesive.

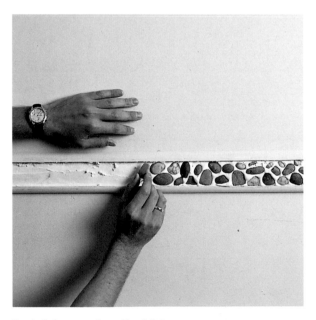

2 Adding the Pebbles
Carefully sink the pebbles into the adhesive until they are held securely. The adhesive should expand to fill the moldings as the pebbles are added. Mop up any spills as you go.

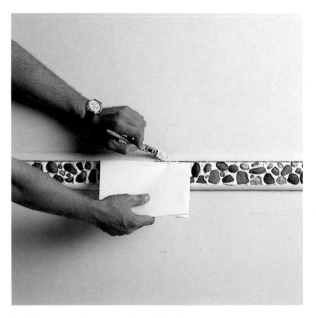

3 Retouching the Molding
When the adhesive is completely dry (after about 24-48 hours), use an artists' brush to retouch any marks on the molding with paint. Use paper or card to protect the pebbles.

Mosaic Pot

Historically, mosaic owes much to the ancient art of inlaying found both in Ancient Egypt and Ancient Mexico, where masks, ornaments and weapons were encrusted with mosaic. Greco-Roman times saw a more naïve and lively style emerge, where loose patterns of shells and stones were common. Our version probably owes more to the evocative art of Antoni Gaudí.

Materials and Tools

Terracotta pot
Fragments of china, glass or tiles
Hammer
Ceramic tile adhesive
Metal spatula

1 Breaking the China
Place your various pieces of discarded china in to a strong plastic bag, seal it, then rest the bag on a hard surface. Use a hammer to gently break the china into manageable pieces.

2 Applying the Adhesive
Spread the ceramic tile adhesive on to the pot with a metal spatula to create an uneven pattern around the rim. Distribute the adhesive evenly to a depth of about ½ in. Work on a relatively small area at a time.

3 Creating a Mosaic
Press the pieces of china firmly into the adhesive to make an interesting pattern. Repeat the process until the whole neck of the pot is covered. Fill any gaps with smaller pieces of china. Leave to set for 48 hours.

String Calico Curtains

This project was devised as a problem-solver rather than a decorative technique, although the end result is rather appealing.

One of the hardest decisions to make when creating a new home is the choosing of soft furnishings. Curtains are a major investment so you should take your time to select the right ones. For these temporary curtains we strung up calico dust sheets, using string as a makeshift curtain heading.

Materials and Tools

Calico cotton cut to fit your window	Sticking tape
	Awl (optional)
Jute string	Hemming tape or
Wooden skewer	latex-based
Cardboard template	household glue

1 Marking the Holes
Fold over 4in of fabric to form a hem and secure with glue or self-adhesive hemming tape. Draw a straight line across the top of the fabric, and using a template, mark out alternate lines of dots.

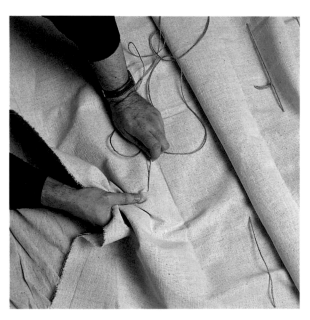

2 Threading the Twine
Fix the string to a wooden skewer with sticking tape and use this, as if it were a needle, to thread the string in lines along the rows of dots on the right side of the fabric to create loops.

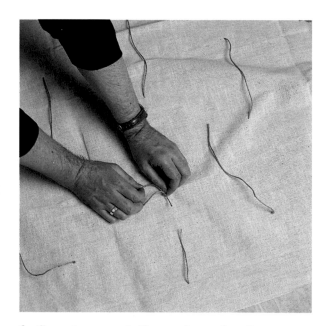

3 Cutting and Knotting the Loops
Turn the curtain wrong side out and cut each loop in the middle. Tie a knot at the top of each piece. Turn curtain over and cut remaining loops. Pull each one as far as it will go and secure with another knot.

String Lampshade and Base

There's something "Out of Africa" about our matching candlestick and lampshade covered with coiled string. Maybe it's because sisal, seagrass and other fibrous materials originate from Africa; or because it's a natural version of the zany kitchen utensils of French West Africa, where colored string is used to wrap everything from ladles to bottle openers.

Undoubtedly though, string is an excellent device for disguising unloved pieces. Ceramic lampbases are perfect for this treatment. Where they were once blushing burgundy or blue in a former life (and positively smacking of an impulsive chain-store buy) they can now sit resplendent in any surroundings.

We've used jute string here, as it is relatively thick, fibrous and has a pleasant natural color. Picture frames and pots are also ideal for this kind of project. Adding a lamp fitting to the candlestick is easy, thanks to special light fittings which have their own cable and just slot into the space where the candle might go. You may find it easier to mark out the pattern on the shade first, by using our paper pattern method shown on page 128.

Materials and Tools

Jute string
White household glue
Clear tape (or masking tape)
Wooden skewer
Awl
Artists' brush

1 Applying the Glue
Make sure your candlestick is clean and dry, then cover the lower half of the candlestick with a generous coat of glue. Use an artists' brush or the manufacturer's spatula.

4 Taping String to Skewer
With clear tape or masking tape, secure the end of the string flush with the end of the kebab stick. This will act like your needle for threading the lampshade.

2 Applying the String

Starting at the rim on the base of the candlestick, gently coil the string around the base and up the stick. Press each coil down firmly and avoid large gaps between the lines as you go.

3 Making Holes in the Shade

Use an awl to make holes in the lampshade about ½ in apart. Work around the top and bottom rim of the shade, until the entire lampshade is punched through. Also punch a few holes in "X" configurations.

5 Blanket Stitch

Thread the string over and under through the two rows of holes to create a blanket stitch effect around the top and bottom rims of the lampshade. Tie a neat knot inside the shade to finish off.

6 Cross Stitching

Fix a new piece of string on to the wooden skewer and sew a few large cross stitches through the pre-marked holes. Knot and tie. For a variation, try different-sized crosses or else small patches of running stitches.

Material Effects

Whether you are inspired by Matisse or Mozart; whether you want color on a grand scale or a quieter, more natural look; whether you can sew or not, the fabulous fabrics on the following pages are yours for the taking ... or possibly faking.

In the next few pages we really put fabric through its paces. From humble dustsheet curtains that are a practical and inexpensive way to dress a window, right up the scale to painted calico and muslin, employing the rich colors of Northern India and the simple textures of dyed and stamped muslin. The only limits are those of your own imagination. Using the simple techniques detailed here you can create your own unique curtains, blinds, cushions and lampshades. Exit the swag, enter the paintbrush.

Fabric Decoration

It all started when we painted a calico curtain with watered-down latex to hide an unattractive doorway. Somewhat surprisingly, the diluted paint doesn't crack when dry; it does stiffen the fabric, but is just fine as a heavy duty curtain or wall hanging, as the photograph opposite shows. Further such forays produced equally inspiring results, so our curiosity was spiked to take the experiments further.

Painted lampshades (page 128) and roller blinds (page 124) were next on the agenda. For the blinds we used ready-primed artists' canvas which provided an unbelievably easy way to make a fully functional and decorative window treatment. Similarly, painted floorcloths (page 126) never seem to tire with age and look wonderful when combined with the simple floor treatments we have devised. All in all, the new home-buyer's dream.

Our great breakthrough came when we discovered that fabric printing inks designed for screen-printing could be diluted with water and used by hand. Suddenly, we had the ability to transform virtually any piece of calico or cotton into any color or shade – armed only with a paintbrush.

Once we had mastered the painting technique, the only hurdle was choosing which colors to use. With a wide-open palette before us, the choice was difficult. To add to the creative process, the paint is colorfast, so it can be further embellished with fabric tapes and rubber stamps in different colors giving you even more options.

Opposite Here's a simple way to hang curtains on a metal or wooden pole without a hint of sewing anywhere. All you need to purchase is an eyelet kit (readily available from any sewing supply store) and some sash-cord rope. This piece of painted calico has been embellished with waterproof markers and literally "strung up" with rope threaded through the eyelets. A painted border adds to the illusion of a printed design and stiffens the edge of the curtain. Quick, easy and inexpensive to achieve, this curtain is the perfect antidote to swags, tails and furbelows.

Painted Fabric

If someone told you that from this point on you had the ability to create fabrics in virtually any color or shade with just a small amount of ink and a paintbrush, would you believe them? Well, it's completely true. All you'll need in addition is a little space, some plastic sheeting and a long table. (Folding wallpaper-pasting tables are ideal for this purpose.)

The fabric paints we've used are actually inks normally used by screen printers for printing on fabric. They are very thick and gloopy to use neat, but mixed with varying amounts of water, they produce wonderful tints and dyes that cover large areas of fabric easily. Once ironed, they are colorfast as well.

We normally dilute one part ink to five parts water – 2 fl oz of dye diluted should give you sufficient liquid to paint 3½ square yards of fabric. Simple designs are the best. Experiment on spare swatches first because, depending on the strength, some colors will run when in contact with others. We are sure you won't be disappointed.

Painted and Dyed Fabric

These instructions outline the basic techniques which will enable you to get used to diluting fabric ink and experimenting with their application. Be guided by your imagination and sketch out color ideas and motifs on paper first. We used calico for this project but any relatively robust cotton fabric would do.

Materials and Tools

Calico
Screen printing ink
4in paint brush
Wallpaper paste brush
Plastic dust sheet
Iron and ironing board
Fabric markers
Waterproof T-shirt pens

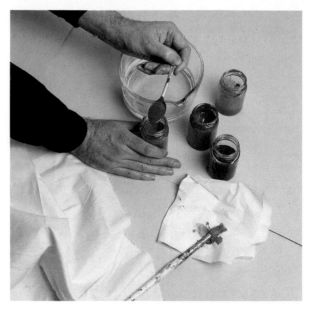

1 Diluting the Ink
Dilute the fabric ink with water to obtain the desired consistency – remember the more water the lighter and less opaque the resulting color will be. Try out your designs on a piece of scrap fabric.

4 Applying the Color
Create depth of color by applying a weaker solution of your chosen tone first and, when dry, follow it with a stronger, darker one. Use a wallpaper paste brush to apply the color over a large area.

2 Testing the Color Tones

Test your chosen color on spare swatches of fabric, as the paints dry to a lighter color than when they are first applied. Make detailed notes on how you mixed each color and tone.

3 Applying the Ink

Always put a plastic dust sheet under the cloth to catch any seepage or splashes. Use a wallpaper paste brush to apply the ink over large areas of fabric. Apply the paint quite liberally.

5 Painting the Stripes

Two-color washed-out stripes can be achieved by applying a second color on top of each stripe while they are still wet. Be careful not to encroach over the striped lines as you work.

6 Fixing and Embellishing

When your work is completely dry, iron the fabric to fix the dye and then embellish it with fine lines applied with waterproof T-shirt pens or fabric markers to create 3-D patterns.

Dyeing and Color Scheming

By diluting our own fabric paints with varying amounts of water, we produced colorfast tones which are infinitely variable. You can experiment with color on scrap pieces of fabric until you achieve the exact tone you require. Not only is it fun to experiment, but your end result will allow you to color-match lampshades, cushions and other soft furnishings to the exact tones of your walls or existing furniture.

Mixing can be just as effective as matching. Here we dyed five lampshades in a variety of summer colors. Simple but effective.

Once you've mastered the art of producing yards of custom-dyed fabric, you can consider embellishing it with a print. In this case our sumptuous Indian-inspired fabric was created using a ready-made rubber stamp dipped in gold paint and embellished with swirls of gold pen.

You could even consider making your own stamp. You just need to trace and cut your design from a thin sheet of rubber and glue this firmly to a wooden block. Indeed, you can use pencil erasers, sponges or even the humble potato to make extremely passable stamps and motifs.

Materials and Tools

Calico
Screen printers' ink
Gold paint
Sash-cord rope
Wallpaper-pasting table
Straightedge
Rubber stamp
Gold marker pen
Iron
Plastic dust sheet
Sewing pins
Sewing thread
White household glue
Eyelet kit
Hammer

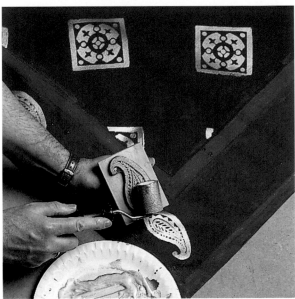

Block-printing is the oldest form of pattern-making and the rubber stamp is its modern-day descendant. A wide range of stamps are available commercially now; to our minds, they're the stencils of the nineties, except that they're re-usable and far more durable.

For this project (see top and opposite), we used gold fabric paint which we applied to the stamp with a small roller. This seems to give the most even coverage. For a unifying effect, we used the same stamping process on our painted floorcloth (above).

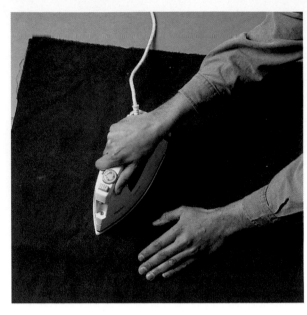

1 Painting the Fabric

Paint on the first coat of diluted fabric ink (see page 112 for proportions) and let it dry completely. Apply the second color in a weaker solution to create a washed out "antique" appearance.

2 Fixing the Dye

When the fabric is completely dry, after a few hours, press the fabric all over with a very hot iron in order to set the dyes and stop them from running if they get wet.

5 Added Decoration

To create a handcrafted finish, embellish the design by applying swirls, dots or other decorative flourishes using a gold marker pen. Alternatively, try silver or gold gilding paste applied with your finger.

6 Attaching the Tape

Make some edging tape by painting a narrow piece of calico (about 2in wide) with gold paint and fraying it along the outer edge. Pin and then machine sew the tape to either edge of the fabric.

3 Marking out the Design

Work out your design and use a straightedge or a scrap piece of wood to mark out a regular repeat on your fabric with a pencil or marker, in preparation for the stamping process.

4 Applying the Stamp

Roll or paint the gold paint onto the rubber stamp, position it above your marker and press down firmly. Repeat until you have stamped the whole piece of fabric with your design.

7 Making an Eyelet Heading

Fold over top edge of fabric by about 4in and glue or sew in position. Use an eyelet kit and a hammer to fix eyelets at regular intervals across the top of the fabric, roughly 4in apart.

8 Fixing the Rope Ties

Thread sash-cord rope or similar thick string through the holes – allowing sufficient rope to form a small loop at each eyelet and knot at each end. The curtain is now ready for hanging.

Painted Furnishings

Painted Roller Blind

To those of us in the non-sewing fraternity, blinds present the ideal solution for providing privacy and keeping out light. However, just like lampshades, their designs seem to veer from rather awful plains to loud, lurid patterns.

Here's an inexpensive idea for a relatively quick-fix solution that can be made to your own designs and is perfectly usable. It has to be said though, that if you plan to adjust the length of your blind on a daily basis, make sure that you're prepared to tie two knots of rope with the same frequency — or alternatively, that you're happy that the blind just rests on the window sill when rolled down — because that is how it works — the blind is held in place by adjustable loops of rope. See page 124 for step-by-step instructions.

Painted Floorcloth

Painted floorcloths, or oilcloths as they were originally known, date back as far as the mid 17th century. They were extremely popular and to this very day make an inspired contribution to any floor. A blank canvas presents a wonderful opportunity for you to make a boldly personal statement — and an inexpensive one at that.

Indeed, in isolation, such freedom of choice could be a problem. Given myriad design options, just where do you start? Color would be a good starting point — after all, the finished item has got to fit in well in its chosen resting place.

Never fear though, inspiration *is* all around us — in books, magazines, films and, of course, in history. Consider then the Scandinavian checkered floor on page 60; recreated on a smaller canvas it would make an ideal floorcloth, simple and elegant. Remember too the other techniques in that chapter — washes of color, faded and distressed borders — the same principles can be applied here to make a covering as authentic or as funky as you wish. See page 126 for instructions on how to make our painted floorcloth.

Painted Lampshade

Lampshades tend to range from the extremely boring to what we call extremely "chi-chi". How many times have you tried to match a lampshade to a particular color scheme or pattern without success? Thankfully, nowadays, more interesting shapes are becoming readily available and they are perfect for painting on your own designs — as elaborate or as simple as you like.

As ever, some of the most effective designs are the simplest ones. A single stripe at top or bottom of a shade can be enough to lift a lamp from oblivion to become a positively vibrant feature in a room. See page 128 for step-by-step instructions.

Opposite A painted roller blind is the perfect solution for small, awkward-shaped windows.

Painted Roller Blind

Somewhat unusually, latex paint is actually ideal for this project as the plastic in it protects the rolled-up fabric and makes it easier to maneuver. If more traditional paints are used, then a coat of spray fixative should be applied when all the paints are dry, and before you fix the blind to the poles.

Materials and Tools

Primed artists' canvas

Latex paint in two colors (we used Provence Blue and Mustard Yellow)

White household glue

Two pieces of ½ in doweling, cut to length

Sash-cord rope or similar

Water-based wood stain

Two large cup hooks

Tenon saw

Staple gun

Scissors

Pencil

Leaf motif template

Motif made from card

Artists' brush

1 in paintbrush

1 Cutting the Canvas
Cut the primed canvas to size. Allow sufficient width to cover the window yet sit comfortably within the frame. There's no need for a hem allowance. Add 8in to the length for fixing to the pole.

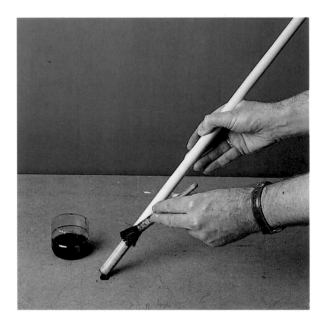

4 Making the Poles
Cut the two ½ in pieces of wooden doweling with a tenon saw to length – approximately 1in wider than the blind itself at either end and paint them with the water-based stain.

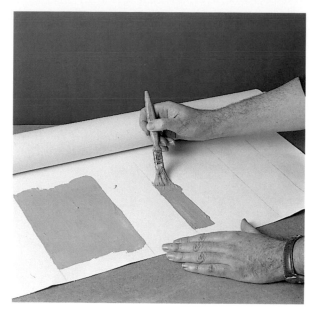

2 Marking and Painting Stripes

Mark out and paint on the stripes in latex paint. Let the first color dry for a few hours. When completely dry, apply the second color which should contrast well with the first.

3 Making the Leaf Design

On the reverse side of the fabric, use a pencil and a leaf template to mark out the design. Paint the outline first and complete the background prior to finishing the individual leaves.

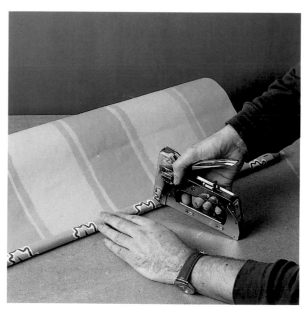

5 Fixing the Blind to Poles

Use glue to attach the fabric to a piece of wooden doweling at each end of the blind and secure in place with a staple gun at both ends. Leave to dry for a period of 4-6 hours.

6 Mounting the Blind

Measure and affix cuphooks into the window frame so that the top pole sits on them comfortably, with space for the ropes as shown. Make loops of rope and roll the blind up to the required length. Then tie them up.

Painted Floorcloth

For our floorcloth we've chosen to pick up on the detail in our Stamped Curtain and Rope Heading (page 120), using a rubber stamp and embellishing it with a gold pen as before.

Materials and Tools

Primed artists' canvas, cut to required size, plus a 1in border

Water-based paint – we used a combination of our New England Red and Jaipur Pink, mixed to make three shades

White household glue or glue gun   Straightedge

Scissors

Gold paint   Two rubber stamps

Water-based varnish   Small roller

Small artists' brush

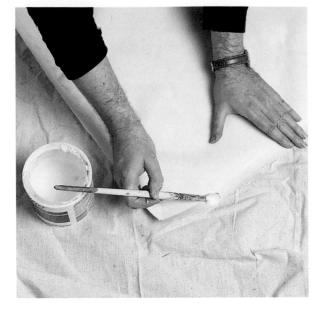

1 Cutting the Cloth to Size

Use a straightedge to mark a 1in border around the cloth and turn under the edges. Cut off the corners to create a mitered edge at each corner. Glue the corners with either a glue gun or white household glue.

2 Painting the Cloth

Paint each color on separately and allow each one to dry before applying the next. We applied a combination of three tones, one around the edge, one on the single border and one in the center panel.

4 Applying the Pattern

Mark the positions of your pattern and stamp out your design, having applied the gold paint with a roller. Use card to mask edges where design bleeds off. Add three coats of water-based varnish to seal in the design.

Painted Lampshade

Our dotty lampshade was painted with our own specialist water-based paint. If you intend to paint the whole shade, apply a small patch of color first and test it with the lamp on to see how opaque the finished result will be.

Materials and Tools

Plain lampshade
Cartridge paper
Water-based paint, Antique White,
  Poppy Red and Pumpkin
Artists' brush
Pencil
Black waterproof marker pen

1 Applying a Base Coat
Paint your lampshade with Antique White. When dry, cover with cartridge paper, tucking in ends. Use a pencil to mark center point of circles at regular intervals, piercing paper and marking lampshade.

2 Painting on the Spots
Use a small artists' brush to apply the Poppy Red spots freehand. If you are unsure about painting these freehand, draw a pencil line around a coin to obtain an exact circle, then paint within the lines.

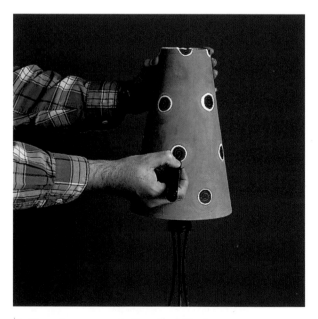

3 Background Embellishment
We painted large circles around each dot using pumpkin paint, then filled in the background with the same color. Use a waterproof marker pen to draw swirls on to the red dots.

Suppliers

Paints and Varnishes

Createx Colors
14 Airport Park Road
East Granby, CT 06026
800-243-2712
Coloring agents for most surfaces, including pearlescents, iridescents, acrylics, fabric colors, pure pigments, liquid dyes

Grand Illusions
2-4 Crown Road, St Margarets
Twickenham, Middlesex
TW1 3EE ENGLAND
181 607 9446
New generation water-based paints, dead-flat varnish, furniture wax, fabric paints, gilding paste

Old-Fashioned Milk Paint Co.
PO Box 222
Groton, MA 01450
617-448-6336
Powder milk paints

Paint Effects
2426 Fillmore Street
San Francisco, CA 94115
415-292-7780
Paint Magic Woodwash colors and other supplies

Pottery Barn retail stores

Tin

Tin for punching (galvanized steel sheeting)

Country Accents
PO Box 437
Montoursville, PA 17754
717-478-4127

Artists' Materials

The Artist's Club
5750 N.E. Hassalo
Portland, OR 97213
800-845-6507
Craft painting materials and supplies, including a wide selection of paints and brushes

Chaselle Inc.
9645 Gerwig Lane
Columbia, MD 2104\
800-242-7355
Brushes, paints, tempera colors, acrylics, pastels, and many other arts and crafts supplies

Chatham Art Distributors
11 Brookside Avenue
Chatham, NY 12037
800-822-4747
Acrylics, brushes, canvasses, oils, milk paint, tin supplies, and wooden items

Natural Fabrics

Coconut Company
129-131 Greene Street
New York, NY 10012
212-539-1940

Homespun Fabrics & Draperies
PO Box 3223
Ventura, CA 93006
805-642-8111

IKEA
1000 Center Drive
Elizabeth, NJ 07202
908-289-4488

Natural Fiber Fabric Club
PO Box 1115
Mountainside, NJ 07092

Color Palettes and Templates

The color palettes on the next few pages will give you an idea of how our new generation of water-based paints perform as blocks of single color and as two-color combinations. Where two colors appear, the top color is listed first.

On pages 138-142 you will find the templates you need for:
Wooden Key Cupboard (page 48),
Ocean Liner (page 52),
Pulp Sculpture Plaque (page 84),
Noah's Ark (page 88),
Punched Tin Cupboard (page 98),

Punched Tin Picture Frame (page 100), Painted Roller Blind (page 124). Either trace over them or photocopy them to your required size.

Color Palettes Key

Page 132
1 Gustavian Blue
2 Mustard Yellow
3 Stockholm Blue
4 Damson
5 Provence Blue
6 Caribbean Green
7 Citrus Yellow
8 Bayberry
9 Adobe Red
10 Forest Green
11 Poppy Red
12 Antique White
13 Barley
14 Pumpkin
15 Caspian Blue
16 Elephant Grey

Page 133
1 Providence Blue
2 Terracotta
3 Moroccan Earth
4 Sorrel
5 Cornflower Blue
6 Buttermilk
7 New England Red
8 Deep Sea Green
9 Eau de Nil
10 Beige
11 Jaipur Pink
12 Apple Green
13 Caribbean Blue
14 Olive Green
15 Fresco Pink
16 Giverny Yellow

Page 134
1 Mustard/Provence Blue
2 Giverny Yellow/Apple Green
3 Fresco Pink/Caribbean Blue
4 Poppy Red/Apple Green
5 Mustard/Apple Green
6 Giverny Yellow/Fresco Pink
7 Fresco Pink/Caspian Blue
8 Poppy Red/Caribbean Blue
9 Citrus Yellow/Caspian Blue
10 Jaipur Pink/Citrus Yellow
11 Pumpkin/Poppy Red
12 New England Red/Olive
13 Citrus Yellow/New England Red
14 Jaipur Pink/Cornflower Blue
15 Pumpkin/Caribbean Green
16 New England Red/Pumpkin

Page 135
1 Caribbean Green/Providence Blue
2 Caribbean Blue/Adobe Red
3 Provence Blue/Mustard Yellow
4 Cornflower Blue/Caribbean Blue
5 Caribbean Green/Fresco Pink
6 Caribbean Blue/Citrus Yellow
7 Provence Blue/Forest Green
8 Cornflower Blue/Poppy Red
9 Sorrel/Adobe Red
10 Apple Green/Poppy Red
11 Caspian Blue/Pumpkin
12 Providence Blue/Apple Green
13 Sorrel/Terracotta
14 Apple Green/Cornflower Blue
15 Caspian Blue/Caribbean Blue
16 Providence Blue/Jaipur Pink

Page 136
1 Elephant Grey/Poppy Red
2 Stockholm Blue/New England Red
3 Olive/Barley
4 Eau de Nil/Providence Blue
5 Elephant Grey/Damson
6 Stockholm Blue/Gustavian Blue
7 Olive/Pumpkin
8 Eau de Nil/Buttermilk
9 Gustavian Blue/Providence Blue
10 Forest Green/Pumpkin
11 Deep Sea Green/Stockholm Blue
12 Bayberry/Terracotta
13 Gustavian Blue/New England Red
14 Forest Green/Apple Green
15 Deep Sea Green/Jaipur Pink
16 Bayberry/Adobe Red

Page 137
1 Antique White/Buttermilk
2 Beige/Gustavian Blue
3 Buttermilk/Pumpkin
4 Barley/Olive
5 Antique White/Provence Blue
6 Beige/Poppy Red
7 Buttermilk/Elephant Grey
8 Barley/Terracotta
9 Damson/Sorrel
10 New England Red/Olive
11 Terracotta/Cornflower Blue
12 Morroccan Earth/Gustavian Blue
13 Damson/Jaipur Pink
14 New England Red/Caspian Blue
15 Terracotta/Giverny Yellow
16 Elephant Grey/Beige

1

2

3

4

5

6

7

8

9

10

11

12

13

14

15

16

1

2

3

4

5

6

7

8

9

10

11

12

13

14

15

16

1 2 3 4

5 6 7 8

9 10 11 12

13 14 15 16

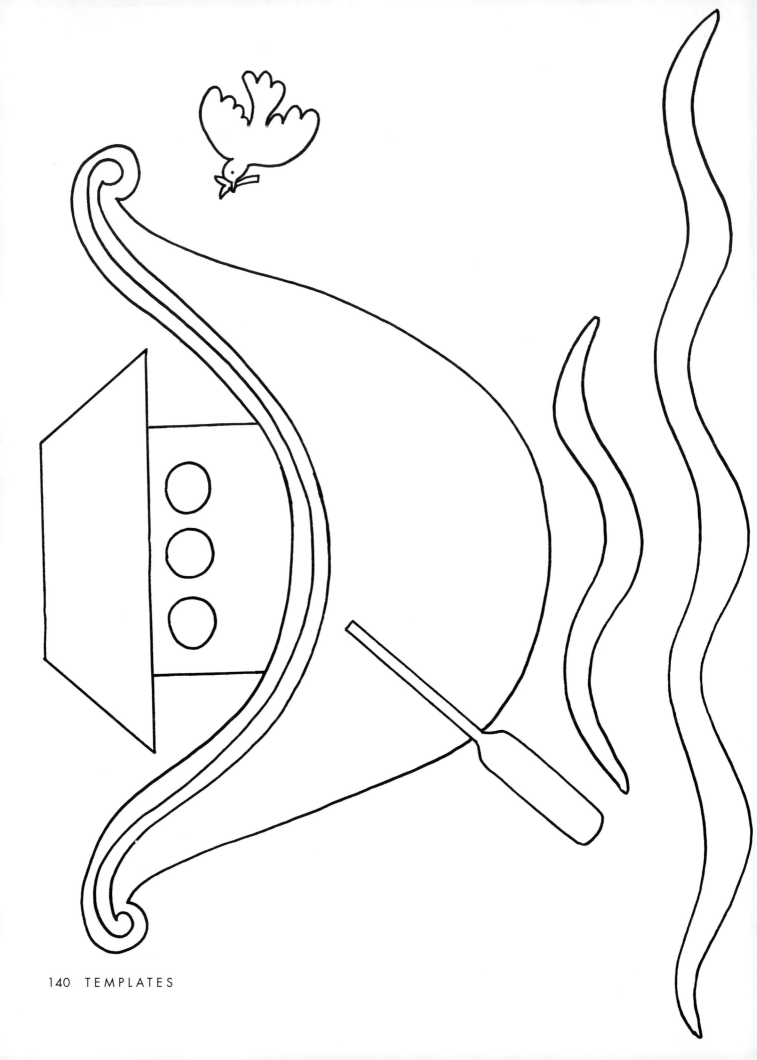

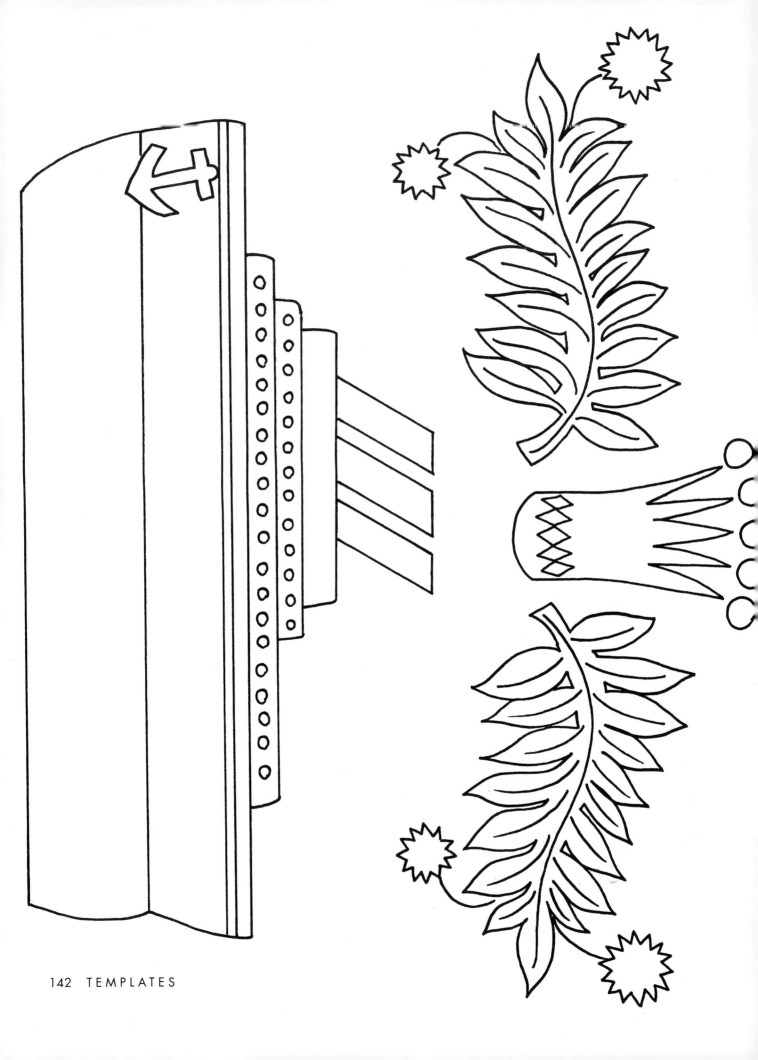

Acknowledgments

This book is dedicated to our dear friend Caroline who died shortly before it was completed, aged 39.

We would like to thank the following people for their invaluable help in the preparation of this book:

Chris Mowe, the unsung hero of the piece, who makes our wonderful paint and whose skill and teaching first inspired us on this path. Denise Bates at Ebury, who had faith in us from day one and who had the courage of her convictions.

David Downie, for his patience, long hours, co-operation, and above all, simply wonderful photography. And not forgetting his tireless assistant, the lovely Miranda – sounds like a circus act if ever there was one!

The multi-talented Lydia Bates, who assisted us on most of the shoots and under whose generous guidance we have developed our fabric paint.

Our small, dedicated team behind the scenes at Grand Illusions, especially Tiggs, Sue, Susan and Marcia, who we had to abandon at times or, worse still, leave to clear up after us.

Laura Anthony who kindly loaned the antique cot on page 86.

To all the customers and friends of Grand Illusions whose kind comments continue to inspire us and without whose support none of this would be possible.

Above all, our greatest and almost immeasurable thanks go to two supremely talented and delightful women – Jo Copestick and Meryl Lloyd. To dear Jo, for making the right calls in the first place, for being so kind and supportive to fledgling authors and for painlessly translating our scrawly writing into legible text. To dear Meryl, for believing in us and planting the right seeds, for constant support and encouragement, guiding us onwards and upwards, and for completely inspirational art direction.

It has been our privilege to work with you all.

Index